JOHN
CALVIN

SPIRITUAL LEADERS AND THINKERS

JOHN CALVIN

DALAI LAMA (TENZIN GYATSO)

MARY BAKER EDDY

JONATHAN EDWARDS

DESIDERIUS ERASMUS

MOHANDAS GANDHI

AYATOLLAH RUHOLLAH KHOMEINI

MARTIN LUTHER

AIMEE SEMPLE McPHERSON

THOMAS MERTON

SRI SATYA SAI BABA

ELISABETH SCHÜSSLER FIORENZA

EMANUEL SWEDENBORG

SPIRITUAL
LEADERS AND
THINKERS

JOHN
CALVIN

Thomas J. Davis

Introductory Essay by
Martin E. Marty, Professor Emeritus
University of Chicago Divinity School

CHELSEA HOUSE
PUBLISHERS
A Haights Cross Communications Company
Philadelphia

COVER: Portrait of John Calvin, c. 1570

CHELSEA HOUSE PUBLISHERS

VP, NEW PRODUCT DEVELOPMENT Sally Cheney
DIRECTOR OF PRODUCTION Kim Shinners
CREATIVE MANAGER Takeshi Takahashi
MANUFACTURING MANAGER Diann Grasse

Staff for JOHN CALVIN

EXECUTIVE EDITOR Lee Marcott
EDITOR Kate Sullivan
PRODUCTION EDITOR Noelle Nardone
PHOTO EDITOR Sarah Bloom
SERIES AND COVER DESIGNER Keith Trego
LAYOUT 21st Century Publishing and Communications, Inc.

A Haights Cross Communications ✦ Company

www.chelseahouse.com

First Printing

9 8 7 6 5 4 3 2 1

Library of Congress Cataloging-in-Publication Data

Davis, Thomas J. (Thomas Jeffery), 1958–
   John Calvin/by Thomas J. Davis.
     p. cm.—(Spiritual leaders and thinkers)
Includes bibliographical references and index.
   ISBN 0-7910-8100-1
   1. Calvin, Jean, 1509–1564—Juvenile literature. 2. Reformation—
Switzerland—Geneva—Biography—Juvenile literature. I. Title. II. Series.
BX9418.D32 2004
284'.2'092—dc22

                                                    2004013706

CONTENTS

Foreword

Why become acquainted with notable people when making efforts to understand the religions of the world?

Most of the faith communities number hundreds of millions of people. What can attention paid to one tell about more, if not most, to say nothing of *all*, their adherents? Here is why:

The people in this series are exemplars. If you permit me to take a little detour through medieval dictionaries, their role will become clear.

In medieval lexicons, the word *exemplum* regularly showed up with a peculiar definition. No one needs to know Latin to see that it relates to "example" and "exemplary." But back then, *exemplum* could mean something very special.

That "ex-" at the beginning of such words signals "taking out" or "cutting out" something or other. Think of to "excise" something, which is to snip it out. So, in the more interesting dictionaries, an *exemplum* was referred to as "a clearing in the woods," something cut out of the forests.

These religious figures are *exempla*, figurative clearings in the woods of life. These clearings and these people perform three functions:

First, they define. You can be lost in the darkness, walking under the leafy canopy, above the undergrowth, plotless in the pathless forest. Then you come to a clearing. It defines with a sharp line: there, the woods end; here, the open space begins.

Great religious figures are often stumblers in the dark woods.

We see them emerging in the bright light of the clearing, blinking, admitting that they had often been lost in the mysteries of existence, tangled up with the questions that plague us all, wandering without definition. Then they discover the clearing, and, having done so, they point our way to it. We then learn more of who we are and where we are. Then we can set our own direction.

Second, the *exemplum*, the clearing in the woods of life, makes possible a brighter vision. Great religious pioneers in every case experience illumination and then they reflect their light into the hearts and minds of others. In Buddhism, a key word is *enlightenment*. In the Bible, "the people who walked in darkness have seen a great light." They see it because their prophets or savior brought them to the sun in the clearing.

Finally, when you picture a clearing in the woods, an *exemplum*, you are likely to see it as a place of cultivation. Whether in the Black Forest of Germany, on the American frontier, or in the rain forests of Brazil, the clearing is the place where, with light and civilization, residents can cultivate, can produce culture. As an American moviegoer, my mind's eye remembers cinematic scenes of frontier days and places that pioneers hacked out of the woods. There, they removed stones, planted, built a cabin, made love and produced families, smoked their meat, hung out laundered clothes, and read books. All that can happen in clearings.

In the case of these religious figures, planting and cultivating and harvesting are tasks in which they set an example and then inspire or ask us to follow. Most of us would not have the faintest idea how to find or be found by God, to nurture the Holy Spirit, to create a philosophy of life without guidance. It is not likely that most of us would be satisfied with our search if we only consulted books of dogma or philosophy, though such may come to have their place in the clearing.

Philosopher Søren Kierkegaard properly pointed out that you cannot learn to swim by being suspended from the ceiling on a belt and reading a "How To" book on swimming. You learn because a parent or an instructor plunges you into water, supports you when necessary, teaches you breathing and motion, and then releases you to swim on your own.

Kierkegaard was not criticizing the use of books. I certainly have nothing against books. If I did, I would not be commending this series to you, as I am doing here. For guidance and courage in the spiritual quest, or—and this is by no means unimportant!—in intellectual pursuits, involving efforts to understand the paths others have taken, there seems to be no better way than to follow a fellow mortal, but a man or woman of genius, depth, and daring. We "see" them through books like these.

Exemplars come in very different styles and forms. They bring differing kinds of illumination, and then suggest or describe diverse patterns of action to those who join them. In the case of the present series, it is possible for someone to repudiate or disagree with *all* the religious leaders in this series. It is possible also to be nonreligious and antireligious and therefore to disregard the truth claims of all of them. It is more difficult, however, to ignore them. Atheists, agnostics, adherents, believers, and fanatics alike live in cultures that are different for the presence of these people. "Leaders and thinkers" they may be, but most of us do best to appraise their thought in the context of the lives they lead or have led.

If it is possible to reject them all, it is impossible to affirm everything that all of them were about. They disagree with each other, often in basic ways. Sometimes they develop their positions and ways of thinking by separating themselves from all the others. If they met each other, they would likely judge each other cruelly. Yet the lives of each and all of them make a contribution to the intellectual and spiritual quests of those who go in ways other than theirs. There are tens of thousands of religions in the world, and millions of faith communities. Every one of them has been shaped by founders and interpreters, agents of change and prophets of doom or promise. It may seem arbitrary to walk down a bookshelf and let a finger fall on one or another, almost accidentally. This series may certainly look arbitrary in this way. Why precisely the choice of these exemplars?

In some cases, it is clear that the publishers have chosen someone who has a constituency. Many of the world's 54 million Lutherans may be curious about where they got their name, who the man Martin Luther was. Others are members of a community but choose isolation: The hermit monk Thomas Merton is typical. Still others are exiled and achieve their work far from the clearing in which they grew up; here the Dalai Lama is representative. Quite a number of the selected leaders had been made unwelcome, or felt unwelcome in the clearings, in their own childhoods and youth. This reality has almost always been the case with women like Mary Baker Eddy or Aimee Semple McPherson. Some are extremely controversial: Ayatollah Ruhollah Khomeini stands out. Yet to read of this life and thought as one can in this series will be illuminating in much of the world of conflict today.

Reading of religious leaders can be a defensive act: Study the lives of certain ones among them and you can ward off spiritual—and sometimes even militant—assaults by people who follow them. Reading and learning can be a personally positive act: Most of these figures led lives that we can indeed call exemplary. Such lives can throw light on communities of people who are in no way tempted to follow them. I am not likely to be drawn to the hermit life, will not give up my allegiance to medical doctors, or be successfully nonviolent. Yet Thomas Merton reaches me and many non-Catholics in our communities; Mary Baker Eddy reminds others that there are more ways than one to approach healing; Mohandas Gandhi stings the conscience of people in cultures like ours where resorting to violence is too frequent, too easy.

Finally, reading these lives tells something about how history is made by imperfect beings. None of these subjects is a god, though some of them claimed that they had special access to the divine, or that they were like windows that provided for illumination to that which is eternal. Most of their stories began with inauspicious childhoods. Sometimes they were victimized, by parents or by leaders of religions from which they later broke.

Some of them were unpleasant and abrasive. They could be ungracious toward those who were near them and impatient with laggards. If their lives were symbolic clearings, places for light, many of them also knew clouds and shadows and the fall of night. How they met the challenges of life and led others to face them is central to the plot of all of them.

I have often used a rather unexciting concept to describe what I look for in books: *interestingness*. The authors of these books, one might say, had it easy, because the characters they treat are themselves so interesting. But the authors also had to be interesting and responsible. If, as they wrote, they would have dulled the personalities of their bright characters, that would have been a flaw as marring as if they had treated their subjects without combining fairness and criticism, affection and distance. To my eye, and I hope in yours, they take us to spiritual and intellectual clearings that are so needed in our dark times.

Martin E. Marty
The University of Chicago

1

Pulled into
the Spotlight

*God having taken me from my originally obscure
and humble condition, has reckoned me worthy
of being invested with the honorable office of
a preacher and minister of the gospel.*

—John Calvin,
*Preface to the Commentary
on the Book of Psalms*

A young man caught up in the religious upheavals of the time made his way to the city of Strasbourg. Protestants controlled the city, and its leaders welcomed those who had turned to this new expression of Christianity. John Calvin, French by birth and one of these new Protestants by choice, had been on the move for quite some time. Having returned to France to settle his affairs after a time in exile because of his newfound faith, he left the country again and headed for a city friendly to his religious perspective. He planned to settle down and continue his private studies and writing, pursuits that suited his shy, intellectual nature. The movement of troops along the roads caused him to detour, however, looping south of his intended destination. He found himself in the city of Geneva, Switzerland, meaning to stay there only a day or so.

Once in Geneva, word of Calvin's presence made its way to William Farel, one of the leaders who had recently helped win the city for the Protestant cause. Farel encouraged Calvin to stay and help with the work in Geneva, but Calvin hesitated. Though his devotion to the cause of religious reform ran deep, he did not think himself suited for such work. He was not ordained and had not studied theology formally, nor had he ever held a position of religious leadership. He would go on to Strasbourg and fulfill his desire to live the life of the private scholar.

Having no luck persuading Calvin to stay, Farel turned to threats. In Calvin's words:

> After having learned that my heart was set upon devoting myself to private studies, for which I wished to keep myself free from other pursuits, and finding that he gained nothing by entreaties, [Farel] proceeded to utter an imprecation that God would curse my retirement, and the tranquility of the studies which I sought, if I should withdraw and refuse to give assistance, when the necessity was so urgent. By this [curse] I was so stricken with terror, that I desisted from the journey which I had undertaken.[1]

In fact, except for a period of just a few years, Calvin would remain in Geneva from the time of his encounter with Farel in August 1536 until his death in 1559. Few historical relationships are as widely recognized as that between the man Calvin and the city of Geneva.

Calvin's identification with Geneva marked him almost as strongly as a book he authored, which was published in March 1536, just a few months earlier. The work carried a very long and ambitious title: *Institutes of the Christian Religion, Embracing Almost the Whole Sum of Piety, and Whatever Is Necessary to Know of the Doctrine of Salvation: A Work Most Worthy to Be Read by All Persons Zealous for Piety.* Though he went on to write many other books, it is this work that became, for so many people, the embodiment of Calvin's religious thought, so much so that it has been said that "Calvin was a man of a single book."[2]

Calvin was 26 years old at the time of the publication of the *Institutes,* and he had published only one other book: a commentary on an ancient Roman thinker named Seneca. In terms of sales and the attention it earned for its writer, the first book was a failure. His second book, however, more than made up for it. Having become known more commonly by its abbreviated title, *Institutes of the Christian Religion,* the work eventually established Calvin as one of the most influential Protestant Christians of the sixteenth century. Indeed, he still stands today as one of the most important religious thinkers in the Western Christian tradition, and the pervasiveness of his ideas can still be found in contemporary American culture. Much of this can be attributed to the *Institutes,* a book that grew with Calvin as he himself matured. Though his goal had been to quietly pursue private studies, his position in Geneva and his *Institutes* pulled Calvin into the spotlight, both in his own century and in the centuries to follow.

The word *piety,* which the *Institutes* emphasizes in its long title, is a word that means religious devotion and duty. Calvin's work presented a way of thinking about how to be a good

Christian: the things one should believe, how one should worship, how to act, and the obligations one has to society. Though the initial 1536 edition may have been meant as a catechism, or summary of religious beliefs, it became as well a defense for "evangelical" Christianity. This is how the early Protestant Christians thought of themselves, as returning to the *evangel*, a word that means *gospel*, which itself means a story of the life and teachings of Jesus. Thus, Calvin's *Institutes* became both an instruction in evangelical Christianity and a defense of it. Calvin reworked and revised his book throughout his life, ending with what is considered to be the definitive Latin edition of 1559. Despite its tremendous growth in size over the years, however, its primary purpose remained the same: to teach true piety. Although, as a book, it was widely read across Europe, it was in Geneva itself that Calvin worked to implement, in a practical and real-life manner, the teachings of the *Institutes*.

A PERIOD OF ANXIETY

Of course, Calvin's work did not appear in a vacuum. By the time his *Institutes* appeared, Christianity had been around for 1,500 years. Furthermore, Calvin ministered most of his life in an area known today as Switzerland, so the tradition to which Calvin belonged was the European tradition, which had long been institutionalized in the form of the Catholic Church. Indeed, since the time of the Emperor Constantine, in the early fourth century, Catholicism and the various European societies were intimately connected. In fact, there had developed the notion of what has been called *Christendom*—the idea that the institutions of Christianity worked with the various machineries of state (kings, princes, dukes, war leaders, etc.) to rule society. Thus, if one considers especially the countries that today make up Western Europe—England, Ireland, France, Spain, Italy, Germany, Austria, Switzerland, the low countries (Holland, Luxembourg, and Belgium), and the Scandinavian countries— one finds in all these places a strong tradition of church and state working together to order society.

Although by Calvin's time a long tradition of Catholic Christianity had embedded itself in Western European society, there was also the sense then and for some time before that things were not quite "right." Calvin's century (the sixteenth, or the 1500s) saw tremendous changes take place; what is more, for well over a century, the church itself had been called into question—not only its role in society, but also its ability to serve the people in such a way as to provide the much hoped for salvation Christianity had traditionally promised. The fact is, many experienced the sixteenth century as an "age of anxiety," and while some of that anxiousness came from social, economic, and cultural factors, a great part of it came from the uncertainty of the religious situation. All factors need to be acknowledged and explored if the rise of Protestantism and Calvin's role in it are to make sense historically.

A variety of factors made the sixteenth century a time of change. In was in this century that European images of the world began to be fundamentally challenged. The old child's rhyme says that "in 1492 Columbus sailed the ocean blue." Columbus found a "new land" to the west, one populated with people who did not look like or think like the Europeans. The tales brought back from the other direction, the East, also began to confront European imaginations, as knowledge of the lands between Europe and India, and on toward Japan and China, grew. At least some in Europe began to question their unique position in the world, and they began to worry about how to square their long-held religious beliefs with traditions obviously different from their own.

Columbus's ships, and the many that followed from other European countries, returned from the Americas with gold and silver. The effect of this influx of new wealth gradually eroded the buying power of the peasants whose lives (and incomes) were tied to a land that did not increase in value. In other words, with the introduction of new money into the economy, one saw in Europe real inflation for the first time in many years. Though only a small percentage (probably 2 or 3 percent per year), the cumulative effect of this inflation over a period of a few decades began to take its toll on the livelihood of people whose existence had always hovered just above bare subsistence. In other words, though the peasants who worked the land labored just as hard as always, what they could buy with their meager incomes shrank. This would lead, over time, to a peasants' rebellion in the 1520s, a movement sparked in part by the ideology of the new religious thought (Protestantism) but also responding to the peasants' deteriorating standard of living.

In addition, during the sixteenth century, there was a "siege" mentality throughout much of Western Europe. Warfare had long been a way of life, and as certain nation states began to form (England, Spain, France), violence often accompanied the consolidation of power. Conflict dogged the smaller territories, as well: The Holy Roman Empire (what would become Germany in the nineteenth century) was a confederation of more than 300 principalities, ranging from city-states to kingdoms the size of modern-day German states (Saxony, for example), and, as the sixteenth century progressed, rebellions and war would continue to break out.

Interestingly, the threat of the sixteenth century that contributed most to this underlying "siege" mentality came from outside Western Europe. The forces of Süleyman the Magnificent, ruler of the Ottoman Empire, an Islamic kingdom centered in the area that today is called Turkey, had pushed his troops far into central Europe; in the 1520s, he was on the doorstep of Vienna. His power continued to grow; he eventually became a major threat in the Mediterranean, and he pillaged Italian cities. The very existence of the Christian West seemed uncertain. People were anxious about their survival culturally, economically, and politically. No wonder that many, including Calvin, perceived themselves to be living in "a world out of joint."[3]

RELIGIOUS UPHEAVAL AND UNCERTAINTY

The bedrock upon which many in Western Europe assumed their society rested was the Catholic Church. For a period of

200 years before Calvin, however, one crisis after another had rocked the church. This gradually led people to question the church's authority to establish the order not just of political affairs but also of religious affairs. The church as an institution had been seen as the guarantor of salvation. The head of the church, the pope, was understood to be the successor of the Apostle Peter, chief of Jesus's disciples. As such, he represented the true faith and teachings of Christianity. The office of pope itself had become problematic in the eyes of many, however, for various reasons.

Though a spiritual ruler, the pope was also a political power, overseeing the administration not only of Rome but also of much of central Italy. Because of political intrigue and power plays, French forces finally overran Rome. They forcibly moved the papacy (the pope and what was required to run his office) to French-controlled territory, to a city called Avignon. There it resided during much of the fourteenth century, from 1309 to 1377.

Because of the perceived "control" of the pope by the French, other countries sought to restore the papacy to Rome. This led to the Great Schism, a period of time during which a pope resided in Avignon and another one resided in Rome. The existence of two popes called into question the validity of the pope's power: Who legitimately spoke for the church? Some began to look to other sources of authority for the final word concerning Christian faith and teaching.

Some leaders and thinkers advocated conciliarism—the idea that the true head of the church was a properly constituted council of the church. Indeed, it was a series of councils in the early fifteenth century that put an end to the Great Schism, finally appointing a pope that would be recognized by all. Once the new pope was in power, however, he and his successors successfully opposed the plans of the conciliarists to control the church. In addition, as the fifteenth century wore on, many people, as well as many church leaders, thought the popes were more interested in political affairs than they were in their spiritual duties. Viewed more as lawyers than pastors, popes began to lose the confidence of people regarding matters of salvation.

Other ideas came forth about that time. Mysticism, the notion that one could unite with God or Jesus in spiritual ecstasy, thus gaining a type of religious authenticity, was an old path increasingly followed by some. As early as the latter part of the fourteenth century and then on into the fifteenth century, still others began to suggest that, in matters of Christian faith and practice, the Bible stood as the final authority, even above the pope. Traditionally, the pope was seen as the one who held the power to interpret the Bible in accord with his office as successor to Peter (according to the Bible, Jesus appointed Peter to be the foundation of his church, and in the Catholic Church, his role as head of the church is seen as being carried out by the pope). Rather than seeing the pope and Bible, or the pope and Peter, as presenting a unified front, though, some now called into question their relationship. Instead of the pope being judge of the Bible, some began to say that the Bible should judge the pope's life and doctrine. By the beginning of the sixteenth century, a book appeared that portrayed a pope's grand procession to the gates of heaven, only to be turned away by Saint Peter himself.[4]

The people of the sixteenth century lived in difficult times. Aside from the changes taking place in society and in the church, they still lived with the remnants of the bubonic plague. The "black death," as it was called, had killed untold hundreds of thousands for 200 years (to learn more about this deadly epidemic, type the keywords "bubonic plague Europe" into any Internet search engine and browse the many websites listed). People in such an environment became obsessed with death. One finds the appearance of books on how to die well; pictures of the "danse macabre" or the "dance of death" filled people's minds. In the midst of such misery, the church had always offered the hope of salvation, saying that the pitiful existence on this earth would not be the final word, but that there would be an afterlife. Now, however, the very institution that had stood for centuries as the vehicle of salvation seemed to be crumbling under the weight of politics, mistrust, misconduct by church officials, and uncertainty. Where could religious authority be found upon which people could rely? For many people of the sixteenth century, that became a burning question.

John Calvin, the shy young man, stepped into the spotlight in 1536 to provide answers.

Growing Up as the World Changes: 1509–1527

The true treasure of the Church is the Most Holy Gospel of the glory and the grace of God.

—Martin Luther, "Ninety-Five Theses"

John Calvin was born in the town of Noyon, France (north-east of Paris), on July 10, 1509. At the time of Calvin's birth, the Catholic Church still held the allegiance, if not always the heart, of Christian Europe. Calvin's family, baptized at birth and carried through life by the sacraments, the sacred rituals of the church, not only professed the Catholic faith but were also financially supported by the church. John's father had worked his way into a position of responsibility at the local cathedral chapter in Noyon (a cathedral housed the seat of a bishop, and a cathedral chapter was the group of clergy that ran the cathedral, usually because the bishop was absent). Through his connections, John's father procured for him a church benefice. Benefices were church offices with duties attached, but by this time it was common for the holder to pay a small portion of the benefice to someone else to perform the duties, while keeping the larger portion for their own financial support. The money from John's benefice would be used for his education.

Very little is known of Calvin's childhood. He left few records that would enable one to reconstruct that time of his life. In this sense, he was like many people of the sixteenth century, or almost any century: The concerns of his adult life—things that he wrote about—were not the sort of things that evoked from him reflections on his childhood. It is known that Calvin's mother died when he was young, perhaps when he was about six years old. He had several brothers, some of whom died very young, and later, a stepmother and stepsisters. In other words, he lived the life of all people in the sixteenth century—a life dogged by constant threats of disease and death.

John's father, however, had worked himself into a position that brought with it benefits not available to all, and he was able to provide for John's education both with his own resources and with those to which he had access through the church. Although little is known of the child John's education, one moves onto more reliable historical ground when Calvin's college years become the subject of inquiry. First, however, it is important to examine two events—one political, that would have religious consequences, the other religious, that would have political consequences—that occurred during Calvin's childhood before he attended college. Both would end up having a profound effect upon Calvin's life.

THE CONCORDAT OF BOLOGNA

The Great Schism that had begun in 1378, wherein two popes (one in Avignon and one in Rome) contested each other's authority, ended in 1417 with the restoration of a single pope, seated in Rome. Whereas it is debated now how much control the French king had over the papacy while it resided in Avignon, apparently the French king thought of a wholly independent papacy as a threat. In 1438, the French clergy issued the Pragmatic Sanction of Bourges, an act that severely curtailed the papacy's power in France. Among other things, it limited the amount of money that went to Rome in church taxes, questioned the pope's right to interfere in the internal affairs of the French church, and declared that a church council stood superior to the authority of the pope. This sanction caused an increase in tensions between the papacy and France.

Nearly 80 years later, in 1516, Francis I, King of France, entered into the agreement known as the Concordat of Bologna with Pope Leo X. Francis had just conquered the Duchy of Milan, and he hoped the agreement with Leo would eventually lead to the pope's support for his political designs on the Italian peninsula. Whereas the Concordat did not help further Francis's cause in Italy, it did increase the power he exerted over the French church.

With the signing of the agreement, Francis revoked the Pragmatic Sanction of Bourges. In return, Leo gave to Francis the right to make appointments in the French church, those appointments then being placed in office by the pope. This gave Francis a level of control over the French church that not all monarchs had in their own countries. Thus, when a religious revolution took place in Europe, Francis had less political reason to support the Protestant cause than did some other rulers, who thought that the papacy exercised far too much control in their respective territories.

In other words, the Concordat of Bologna presented Francis I with a strong political incentive to support the institution of the Catholic Church while discouraging the growth of Protestantism within his kingdom. As the years passed, discouragement took the more extreme forms of persecution and execution. The political Concordat gave Francis good reason to keep his country Catholic.

THE BIRTH OF PROTESTANTISM

If the Concordat of Bologna provided an important political milestone that would affect young Calvin as he moved from childhood into his college years and beyond, the upheaval known as the Protestant Reformation would claim Calvin's religious loyalty. Exile from his homeland would be the eventual result.

There had long been calls for religious reform throughout Catholic Europe. Although some saw the conciliar movement as a way to accomplish reform, others looked beyond the council to something else: the Bible. For more than 100 years before the birth of Calvin, individuals appeared who called on Christians to look to the Bible as the ultimate source of religious authority, above and beyond the institutional church, whether that institution was represented by the pope or by a church council.

None of those individuals, however, had created movements that effectively challenged the position of the Catholic Church. That changed when a monk named Martin Luther began to question the authority of the church.

Martin Luther lived in the Holy Roman Empire, in an area then called Electoral Saxony. Today, that territory is in the northeastern part of Germany. Martin Luther was German by birth, spoke German, and his initial appeal was to those German-speaking people within the Holy Roman Empire.

What became a decisive break with the Catholic Church started simply enough. Luther created a document known as the "Ninety-Five Theses." Written in Latin, the language of the learned, Luther intended an academic debate on issues related to salvation, the role of the church in salvation, and the notion of God's grace. In October 1517, Luther posted these theses in Wittenberg, the town in which he lived. Someone stole the document, had it translated into German, and then distributed it.

A MONK'S SQUABBLE

Monks are those who set their lives apart from the ordinary world to pursue a life of prayer. There developed in Western Christianity many such groups of monks, who lived in places called monasteries. Individual monasteries were usually part of a larger network, with monasteries within this larger group following the same guidelines. Monasteries were thus distinguished by the religious rule they followed. There were many different religious orders. Oftentimes, they competed with one another; sometimes, they fell into open conflict.

Martin Luther belonged to an Augustinian monastery; that is, they followed the Rule of St. Augustine. It was in this place that Luther had his conversion experience, and he came to believe that a Christian is saved solely by faith apart from good works. He sought to incorporate this insight into his religious life, then he began to share it with others.

In 1517, a monk from another religious order, the Dominicans, came near to where Luther lived, selling indulgences. An indulgence forgave the earthly penalty associated with the forgiveness of sin (the way the system of penance worked, one confessed sin, was forgiven, then was assigned a penalty to perform to show true repentance). By the time of Luther, however, the selling of indulgences was sometimes used to raise money. The common people thought of it as "buying" forgiveness. This, of course, struck at the heart of Luther's newfound belief that salvation was received by grace alone apart from any good works performed by the believer.

Luther hotly contested the work of the Dominican indulgence seller, a man named John Tetzel. In response, Luther posted the "Ninety-Five Theses," traditionally seen as the starting point of the Reformation. At first, the hierarchy of the church ignored the conflict, and Luther's growing popularity and sense of outrage, simply seeing the conflict, not as a matter of the very salvation of souls, but as a monks' squabble—the usual fighting between two different religious orders.

As Luther debated on topics related to salvation and grace, his central concerns, his fame grew. His primary point concerned the role of faith in salvation. He believed that a Christian attained salvation through God's grace alone and that grace was received by the Christian through faith in God. Luther taught that it was such faith that was saving, not the good works a person did. He believed truly good works only followed the outpouring of God's grace; good works could not be the cause of God giving grace to the Christian.

Luther's opinions came under close scrutiny by the authorities of the Catholic Church. Finally, the hierarchy of the church, the pope and his advisors, decided to excommunicate Martin Luther. In the sixteenth century, excommunication meant both that one was excluded from the ministrations of the church and that one was an outlaw in the eyes of the civil society. There was no separation of church and state at that time.

Having heard that the document that would either call for him to recant what he had taught or be excommunicated from the church was on its way to him, Luther spent a very busy summer writing several treatises that would become known as the "Reformation Treatises." One was pastoral in tone and explained a Christian's religious duty. One was theological, and it attacked the sacramental system of the church. The sacraments were the rituals the church used to signify important events in a Christian's life; indeed, the church taught that these sacraments were vessels of God's saving grace. The church held that there were seven sacraments (baptism, confirmation, marriage, holy orders, penitence, communion, and extreme unction); Luther disagreed, saying there were only three that had the authority of Jesus behind them, and then he eventually scaled even that number down to two (baptism and communion). Finally, he penned "An Address to the German Nobility," calling on the individual rulers of the Holy Roman Empire to reform the church, especially since the administration of the church (the papacy) was not able to reform itself.

Though the story of Martin Luther is an interesting one, it is enough to say that, after a confrontation with representatives of the church and an appearance before the Holy Roman Emperor himself, the church excommunicated Luther with the support of the emperor. The movement he had started was what became known as Protestantism, and it could not be stopped. Many of the nobles of the Empire, including Luther's own local ruler, Prince Frederick, sided with Luther. The Holy Roman Empire is thus the first area in Europe to be torn apart by religious differences. Part of the empire became Protestant; part remained Catholic. There would be intermittent warfare throughout the sixteenth century because of these religious disagreements.

Thus, a religious event—the development of a new religious consciousness in the person of Martin Luther—eventually led to political outcomes: war and the splitting of Europe into Protestant and Catholic kingdoms.

YOUNG CALVIN ATTENDS UNIVERSITY

The enactment of Concordat of Bologna and the posting of Luther's "Ninety-Five Theses" occurred in 1516 and 1517, respectively, when Calvin was seven, then eight, years old. He would finish growing up in what would become an increasingly religiously divided Europe. By the time he made a choice for religious reform as a Protestant, which, as a French citizen, carried for him political consequences, he was in his twenties and the Reformation movement was an established cause. In other words, although he was an early Protestant, he was not what is known now as a first-generation reformer. He was what has come to be called a second-generation reformer because he was born about a generation after such first reformers as Martin Luther. Whereas the first-generation reformers paved the way for Protestantism initially, people such as Calvin helped to consolidate the work of those who had come before them.

Before that could happen, however, young John would have to grow up. In 1523, when he was about fourteen years of age, Calvin moved to Paris.[5] At that time, the University of Paris comprised numerous colleges, and there is some uncertainty about where Calvin may have initially enrolled. Regardless, he soon transferred to the Collège de Montaigu and embarked upon the study of the liberal arts, which in most sixteenth-century universities meant the study of philosophy. This could only come after a student had prepared himself well enough in Latin, because that was the language of learned society and the language in which the school books were written.

The curriculum required several years of work, during which students studied logic and especially the work of Aristotle, together with commentaries on the subjects. This first degree in the arts (philosophy) stood as a prerequisite to the study of the "higher" disciplines: theology, law, and medicine.

Calvin's father sent him to school with the intention that he would study theology. This seemed a natural course of advancement for John, given his father's position with the church.

At about the time Calvin had completed his work in liberal arts—1527 or 1528—his father decided he should study law instead of theology. Calvin suggests that the reason for the shift was financial: More money could be made in civil law (as opposed to canon law, which is church law) than in theology. It may also be, however, that the financial irregularities of which his father would be accused had already begun to be a problem, and Calvin's father realized that the advancement of his son in the church might be jeopardized because of the brewing controversy.

In the late 1520s, Calvin moved to Orléans to study with the law faculty. Calvin then came into contact with a new way of learning and thinking. If at Paris he had studied philosophy, especially as it had been filtered through late medieval thought, he now began to learn about a new approach to knowledge based less on what Calvin came increasingly to think of as the "vain speculations" of philosophy and more on ancient writings and authorities. During law school, Calvin encountered humanism.

HUMANISM

Although the word *humanism* can have many meanings, in the sixteenth-century context it refers to a way of thinking that valued ancient authorities over more modern ones, and it emphasized learning the languages of antiquity in order to reach the sources of authoritative knowledge. Humanists believed that there had once been a more "pure" source of knowledge and a better language for expressing that knowledge and that the intervening centuries had added unhelpful layers of opinion written in an increasingly barbaric style of Latin.

Thus, many humanists looked back to what they considered the "font" of their civilization —ancient Greece and Rome. Humanists exhibited a "golden age" mentality, and they looked to ancient philosophy, letters, art, and architecture to help them retrieve something they thought had been lost with the passage of time. For example, one of the great books of Renaissance art (one must remember that the great artist Michelangelo and the great reformer Martin Luther were contemporaries), Alberti's *On Drawing*, which served in many ways as the Renaissance textbook on painting, drew heavily on ancient writers and their theories of mathematics and art. With regard to language, many humanists looked back to the great Roman orator Cicero, who had lived over 1,500 years earlier, as the best guide to mastering the Latin language.

Finally, there emerged a phenomenon referred to now as "Christian humanism." It had many of the same concerns and impulses as humanism, but its focus was on the Christian faith. Thus, the Bible, especially the New Testament, became very important as the "source" or "font" of Christian life; much effort went into finding the oldest available manuscripts and creating the best possible Greek New Testament from those manuscripts. Mastery of Greek became a cornerstone of Christian humanism. Along with the New Testament itself, the early Christian writers were seen to have lived in the "Golden Age" of the church, so the earliest commentators on the Bible gained a position as authoritative interpreters. Some of these early Christian writers wrote in Greek, and a little later in time, Latin. As in the humanist movement, the Christian humanists schooled themselves in Greek and Latin so that they could read the sources of the earliest Christian tradition, which they considered the most authoritative.

This ideal would be absorbed by Calvin and used by him to great effect once he committed himself to the cause of reform.

3

From Lawyer to Protestant Reformer: 1528–1535

... I may promise this much, that [the Institutes of Christian Religion*] will be a kind of key opening up to all the children of God a right and ready access to the understanding of the sacred volume. . . . And since we are bound to acknowledge that all truth and sound doctrine proceed from God, I . . . acknowledge[d] it to be God's work rather than mine. To him, indeed, the praise due to it must be ascribed.*

—John Calvin, Preface to the 1545 French edition, *Institutes of the Christian Religion* alvin studied law at two universities: Orléans and Bourges. At both places, the spirit of humanism enveloped him. Both universities emphasized the foundations of the Roman legal system and its code of law. Whereas Calvin started at Orléans, he moved to Bourges when that university attracted a famous Italian humanist to its law faculty, a man named Alciati. He then, later, decided to go back to Orléans to finish his legal education.

Calvin became a competent lawyer because of his work at these two schools. It is clear that he exercised his legal training later in life. He learned more than the practical application of law, however; he also developed habits of thought that would be of great advantage to him later, in his work as a Protestant reformer.

At the heart of the Protestant enterprise stood the Bible and its role in faith and doctrine. As Alister McGrath has said:

> The origins of Calvin's methods as perhaps the greatest biblical commentator of his age lie in his study of law in the advanced atmosphere of Orléans and Bourges. There is every indication that he learned . . . the need to be a competent philologist, to approach a foundational text directly, to interpret it within the linguistic and historical parameters of its context, and to apply it to the needs of the present day.[6]

Calvin graduated from Orléans in 1531, and by the summer he had moved back to Paris. He apparently hoped to make his mark there as a humanist scholar. He finished a commentary on an ancient Roman text, Seneca's *On Clemency*, and self-published it in April 1532. Not only did the book not bring Calvin recognition as a humanist scholar, but it also turned out to be a financial disaster for him. He ended up having to borrow money from friends.

Not much is known about Calvin's life over that next year. He left Paris not long after the publication of his book and went back to Orléans—whether to study, work, or teach is not certain. Then, after a little more than a year, Calvin is known to have attended a meeting in his native Noyon in

August 1533. Two months later, he was back in Paris. The atmosphere was volatile.

A THEOLOGICAL CONTROVERSY
AND ITS CONSEQUENCES

The theological faculty in Paris spoke out vehemently against both the reform movement of Luther and humanism. They especially thought the call to study the Bible in its original languages unnecessary.

On the other hand, the faculty seemed to be out of favor with the king, Francis I. They were at odds with one another on a variety of theological and political issues. What is more, Francis appeared to prefer a type of moderate reform of the church (a spiritual reform from the inside by those committed to the church). This does not mean that Francis in any way favored the type of reform taking place in the Holy Roman Empire in those territories where princes had supported Lutheranism.

It may have been that Francis's outlook was misread by some who hoped for evangelical reform in France similar to that promoted in Luther's teachings. In the fall of 1533, a man by the name of Nicholas Cop had been elected rector of the University of Paris. He gave his inaugural speech on November 1, 1533.

The speech caused a sensation. He embraced moderate reform, drawing on the Christian humanist Erasmus and on Luther, but the call to reform was not a radical one. Still, given the environment in Paris at the time, it caused a firestorm. Cop was dismissed as rector. The French Parliament called him to appear before them. Cop escaped Paris, and King Francis I ordered the arrest of the person who allowed him to escape. What is more, action was taken against several individuals who were thought to have Lutheran sympathies. Calvin would certainly have been among their number had he remained. But he did not stay—he fled the city. The authorities searched his room and took his papers.

Historical evidence is ambiguous as to the authorship of Cop's address. Some think Calvin wrote it, or at least had a hand in writing it. Whether he did or did not, however, Calvin clearly stood close enough to Cop to think himself in danger.

During the rest of 1533 and all of 1534, Calvin moved around quite a bit. In May of 1534, he went to Noyon and resigned the positions he held in the Catholic Church that had supported him while he went to school. Everyone agrees that, by this time, Calvin had had a conversion experience that placed him firmly

A "NEW" NEW TESTAMENT

In 1516, Erasmus of Rotterdam published his Greek New Testament. As a humanist and a Christian, Erasmus had great interest in the sources of early Christianity. He pulled together what Greek manuscripts of the New Testament he could find and then edited the material to produce his work.

For more than 1,000 years, the Catholic Church used a version of the Bible called the Vulgate, which was translated by St. Jerome in the fifth century. It was called the Vulgate because Jerome translated Greek and Hebrew texts into Latin, which was then the "vulgar" (common) language. Because of the humanists' interest in recovering original sources, Erasmus undertook the production of the Greek New Testament. His work became the foundation for other work, especially that of translation; during the time of the Reformation, Protestant scholars sought to make the Bible available in the language of the people. Martin Luther, for example, translated the New Testament from Greek into German in the early 1520s.

One example of the difference this new resource made can be found in the Gospel of Matthew. At 4:7 in the Latin Vulgate, Jesus says, "Do penance." Penance was a particular rite of the Catholic Church—a sacrament that involved confessing sins to a priest. As a result of Erasmus's work, it became clear that the passage should be translated as "Repent!" In other words, the command of Jesus had less to do with a church ritual and more to do with making changes in one's life.

Though Erasmus himself remained Catholic, many Protestants used his work both to attack the practices and beliefs of the Catholic Church as unbiblical and to build constructive systems of thought and worship practices they considered to be true to the Bible.

Calvin would come to rely heavily on Erasmus's New Testament the more he dealt with interpreting the Bible.

on the side of the Protestants. In October, there occurred the affair of the placards, notices that were put up in some of the main towns of France. The work of Protestants, these posters attacked the Catholic way of celebrating communion, the sacred reenactment of Jesus's last supper with his disciples, something that stood at the heart of Christian worship. One had even been posted on the king's chamber door. Reaction was swift. By November, over two hundred arrests had been made. Executions took place steadily over the next three months; early in 1535, one of Calvin's friends was burned as a heretic.

In January 1535, Calvin fled to Basel, Switzerland. Except for a few brief excursions, he would live the rest of his live in exile from his homeland.

The 1536 *Institutes*

During the brief time he was in Basel, Calvin completed his *Institutes of the Christian Religion* (whether he wrote the entire book while in Basel or whether he had already started it earlier and simply finished it there is debated). The dedication page is dated September 10, 1535, and publication came in March 1536.

Calvin began the book as a catechism, that is, as an elementary instruction in the faith of the evangelical Christians. Many church reformers used the word *evangelical* to describe themselves. They understood themselves to have returned to the evangel. (The Greek word *evangelion* is translated into English as "gospel," and these evangelicals understood the teachings of and about Jesus to comprise the gospel; of course, the word is found in the titles of the New Testament books that tell about Jesus: the gospels of Matthew, Mark, Luke, and John).

Evangelicals used the gospels to attack the perceived abuses of the Catholic Church while also using these books, along with others in their Bible, as the standard to judge true Christian teaching. Traditionally, the pope and bishops were understood to be the ones who spoke authoritatively on matters of Christian life and faith. Reformers claimed, however, that centuries of human additions and traditions had been added to the teaching of Scripture (a word some use to refer to the Bible), hence the church had suffered moral and doctrinal decline.

Calvin originally meant for his book to aid in teaching what should be considered "biblical." Calvin perceived the work to be a "simple and . . . elementary form of teaching."[7] Because of the political turmoil in France, however, Calvin decided to present his work as a confession of faith to the King of France, Francis I, and thus addressed him directly in the opening of the book: "To the most mighty and most illustrious monarch Francis, most Christian king of the French, his esteemed prince and lord, John Calvin sends peace and greeting in the Lord."[8]

Once he had given his greeting, Calvin began to argue on behalf of the persecuted evangelicals in France and refuted charges that the teachings of reformers were "new." He contended, instead, that the substance of evangelical teaching lay within Scripture itself. In essence, to attack the tenets of evangelical faith bore the consequences of attacking Scripture itself as the Word of God. Calvin ended his dedicatory letter by warning the king that the innocent, faithful followers of God's Word would receive, finally, divine vindication.

This episode is a clear reminder that, in sixteenth-century Europe, church and state were not kept separate. The two were, in the minds of most, irrevocably intertwined. Indeed, many saw the joining of church and state as God's will. Thus, many reformers, including Calvin, would call upon the rulers and governing bodies to do what they believed to be their duty: protect, preserve, nourish, and strengthen true religion.

After the dedicatory letter in the 1536 *Institutes,* six chapters follow. The first chapter is an explanation of "The Law," meaning here the religious law: the Ten Commandments found in the Bible. Much of what would characterize Calvin in his mature theology is sketched out there. This first chapter is very important as a guide to how Calvin's theology developed over the course of his lifetime.

Calvin believed that all true teaching, or doctrine, was contained in the knowledge of God and the knowledge of self.

According to Calvin, God is infinite in power, wisdom, righteousness, and glory. God created the world, and all within it should serve God's glory. Additionally, God is a just judge, taking vengeance on those who take away from God's glory. Finally, God is merciful, willing to forgive and to take back those who trust in God.

Humanity, according to Calvin, who drew upon long established teachings of the tradition of Christianity, was created in the image of God, yet it turned away from God, choosing instead evil. Thus, although humanity is obligated to serve God's glory, it does not.

Calvin argued that all humans know the depth of their disobedience. Everything one should do is inscribed in the natural law and lodged in a person's conscience. God went further and created the written law, the Ten Commandments, as a witness to this natural law. Like Martin Luther, Calvin understood the function, finally, of this written law this way: to teach that "God is the Creator, our Lord and Father. For this reason we owe him glory, honor, and love. Since, however, not one of us performs these duties, we all deserve the curse, judgement—in short, eternal death. Therefore we are to seek another way to salvation than the righteousness of our own works. This way is the forgiveness of sins."[9]

The law, in other words, presents what is necessary for humanity to do to glorify God. It also serves as a mirror, however, of how far humanity falls short in fulfilling this obligation. Thus, the law reveals two things: what humans must do to please God, and the fact that they cannot do so.

The solution to this problem, according to Calvin, is to turn to Christ and the forgiveness of sins God makes available through him. For Calvin, this was the only means of salvation: One had to rely on Christ's mercy rather than one's own goodness and good works if one were to ever be acceptable to God.

After having made these points, Calvin turned to an explanation of the Ten Commandments, treating each individually (for more information on the commandments, enter the keywords "ten commandments bible" into any Internet search engine and browse the sites listed). Then, in summary, he asserted that the whole purpose of the law pertained to love: love of God and love of neighbor. Calvin thought, in the end, that one could make three uses of the law: (1) as a mirror by which one came to see oneself as sinful in nature, thus causing one to turn to the mercies of God; (2) as a guide for the larger society in setting up constraints on the wickedness of people (do not kill, do not steal, etc.); and (3) for Christians, as an exhortation to do good, not in the sense that so doing contributed to salvation, but in the sense of having experienced God's salvation through Christ, Christians would seek to express their gratitude through their actions.

Other chapters follow. The second deals with the notion of faith: both in the content of Christian faith (and on this Calvin turned to an ancient statement of Christian belief, the Apostles' Creed) and faith itself. Although it is important to know what one believes (hence the explanation of the Creed), there is more to faith, for Calvin, than simply "believing." True faith is putting "all hope and trust in one God and Christ, and to be so strengthened by this thought, that we have no doubt about God's good will toward us." [10]

Chapter 3 examines the Lord's Prayer ("Our Father, who art in heaven . . ."), analyzing each of the six petitions in the prayer. Moreover, Calvin looks at the reasons why Christians pray and discusses the practice of prayer.

Chapters 4 and 5 deal with the sacraments of the church. Seven sacraments had developed in Catholic Christianity: baptism, confirmation, communion (the ritual re-enactment of Jesus's last supper using bread and wine, which can also be known as the Eucharist, the Lord's Supper, and the Last Supper), penance, marriage, holy orders, and last rites. Following what had become common among most Protestants, Calvin focused on baptism and the Eucharist as what he considered the true sacraments, while arguing that the other five should not be considered sacraments at all and should be discarded.

The sacraments (most especially the Eucharist) are examined at length in a later chapter. As much as anything, how the different Christian groups understood the sacraments separated them from one another, oftentimes with terrible consequences. Calvin had come to accept the notion that baptism and the Eucharist alone were sacraments. Also, in this early writing, he already has a notion of "accommodation" at work: the idea that, since people are physical as well as spiritual beings, God accommodates his message to human senses. Thus, as well as hearing the Word of God spoken, Christians have the visible signs of the sacraments set before them, to help them in their weakness understand what God wants to say.

The final chapter, chapter 6, treats Christian freedom, ecclesiastical power (meaning that of the church), and civil government. Herein Calvin examines the proper understanding of the free conscience; the role of the church understood in its true sense—that place where God is with his people; and the state, whose purpose is to order society—to provide for the general well-being and safety of those subject to the government.

This relatively small book would grow over the years to many times its original size. And as the book grew, so did its author's reputation and influence. It was the initial small work by which Farel and others in Geneva judged Calvin initially fit for leadership. Indeed, it would be the book, reworked over his lifetime, by which the larger world would come to judge Calvin, at least as a theologian of international and enduring importance. That lay in the future, however. In early 1536, Calvin found himself on the road again.

4

Learning to Be a Leader: 1536–1541

He who through faith is righteous shall live.

—Romans 1:17

C alvin traveled with a friend from Basel to Ferarra, Italy, to the Duke of Ferarra's court (his friend was well connected). Little is known of his stay there. In April 1536, a religious scandal related to matters of reform broke out. Arrests were made, but Calvin had already made his exit. He went back to Basel for a brief time, then traveled to France. By the time he got there in early June, King Francis I had issued a decree that allowed exiles to come back to the country upon the condition of reconciling with the Catholic Church within six months.

Calvin took this time to settle some legal affairs related to his parents' estate, but he remained less than three months. By August, he and a party that included some of his family headed toward Strasbourg, a city known for it openness to the new evangelical faith of the Lutherans and other like-minded religious reformers. Because of troop movements along the way, Calvin never made it. Instead, he found himself in Geneva, and as recounted in chapter one, it was there that William Farel convinced Calvin to stay and help with the work of reforming the church.

Within the short span of a few years, Calvin would find himself called to ministry in Geneva, kicked out of the city, and then called back. These years saw the production of important works from Calvin   mature beyond his years and training— meant to educate Christians and organize the church. Calvin's interpretation and application of these writings also exhibited his sometimes uncompromising personality, which would be the source of his expulsion from Geneva. His intellect had been trained in the university; the leadership he first exhibited in Geneva, however, was underdeveloped for the task at hand. He would not be the first person of brilliance to fail at his first real job.

REFORM IN GENEVA

Farel had been at the task of reform before Calvin arrived. As so often is the case during this time in history, religious change came through those who ruled. In Saxony, where Luther lived, a single ruler named Frederick reigned. With Frederick's support, Luther embarked on the task of changing the structure, worship, and theology of the church in Saxony.

The situation in Geneva mirrors that of many cities that moved in favor of religious reform. For hundreds of years, the city had been ruled by a bishop-prince, usually from the house of Savoy, a nearby French principality. (Geneva was and is a French-speaking city, located in modern-day Switzerland.) In the early sixteenth century, Geneva began to chafe under Savoyard rule (to learn more about these monarchs, enter the keywords "'house of savoy' italy" into any Internet search engine and browse the sites listed). Consequently, there arose a faction who wanted to make the city and its surrounding territory an independent republic.

In trying to throw off Savoyard control, those in favor of Genevan independence had good reason to want to weaken the control and authority of the bishop. Thus, at least in part, the adoption of evangelical attitudes was as political as it was religious. Although those involved in the spread of Reformation ideas may have been especially concerned with the religious aspect of reform, they contributed through their work to the fall of the Catholic Church in Geneva, not just as a religious institution but as a political institution as well, for the bishop was both a religious and a political authority figure. As one scholar of the Reformation in Geneva says, "The overthrow of the Bishop meant that Geneva's rulers had made an irrevocable break with the old faith."[11]

Geneva gained freedom (with the help of its ally, Berne, a city that had already adopted the Reformation) in early 1536. The ultimate political authority now lay with the councils. These councils had existed for many years, but their authority had always been tempered by the bishop-prince of Savoy. Now Geneva ruled itself through its system of councils. In other words, Calvin walked into a city that had just freed itself from the rule of a religious figure and an outsider. Those who looked after Geneva's interests would have no interest in once again turning control of the city over to a religious figure and an outsider. The council meant to control both city and church.

Again, religious reform had been helpful to the political needs of those who sought Genevan independence. That reform would now proceed, but under the watchful eye of the council.

Hence, Calvin walked into a highly volatile situation. There

GENEVAN COUNCILS

For the purpose of simplicity, this text always refers to "the council" when it speaks of Calvin's relationship to the ruling authority of Geneva. In fact, however, Geneva had three councils. They were inter-related, but they each had distinctive roles to play in governing Geneva.

Usually, when the word *council* is used in the text, it means the Little Council (sometimes referred to as the Small Council or the Senate). This is the group before which Calvin most often appeared, and it is the group that saw to the day-to-day running of Geneva. It consisted of 25 members, 4 of whom served as syndics (administrative heads).

In addition, there was the Council of Sixty. It was composed of the Little Council (with 25 members) and another 35 councilors. The Council of Sixty dealt primarily with diplomatic issues.

The 35 additional councilors added to the Little Council to make up the Council of Sixty were drawn from the Council of Two Hundred. This council approved legislation drawn up by the Little Council, and it also elected members to that council.

The General Assembly consisted of all eligible voters in Geneva. All male citizens could vote and hold seats on any of the three councils. Bourgeois were people, not citizens, who had been granted special status by the Small Council or who had bought that position. They could vote as part of the General Assembly and hold seats on the Council of Two Hundred and the Council of Sixty. Finally, there were habitants, who could neither vote nor hold public office, except for pastor or lecturer. They could be easily dismissed from their positions and exiled by the Little Council.

For all but the last five years of his life, John Calvin was a habitant in the city of Geneva.

were factions within the city; some were pro-independence, whereas others favored Savoy influence. Some favored religious reform, but others did not. Even among the ones who favored reform, there was disagreement over how to proceed.

By January 1537, Calvin had been installed by the city council as a Reader in Holy Scripture. Later, he was appointed pastor. It should be noted that Calvin was installed not by ecclesiastical authority but by the civil authority.

He went about his tasks of preaching and teaching from the Bible. In January 1537, Calvin and Farel presented articles for the organization of the church in Geneva to the city council. These guidelines called for the celebration of the Lord's Supper every month (Calvin thought it best celebrated every Sunday, but he recognized that this might be too much, given the tradition of lay people participating in the sacred meal only once per year); Genevans were to subscribe to a confession of faith that had been drawn up earlier by Calvin and Farel; the church should have congregational singing (psalms); and a catechism was to be drawn up to teach the children the fundamentals of the faith.

There were other provisions. One of the most important was the notion of *excommunication*, which literally means "outside the communion." For those who lived in open sin, the articles provided that they should not be able to participate in the Lord's Supper, though they should still come to the preaching so they might learn to mend their ways.

The councils approved these articles, except for the celebration of the Lord's Supper. Instead, the sacred meal would be offered once per quarter (every three months) in each parish church. Thus, the path toward continuing reform in the church of Geneva appeared to be straight and clear.

CONFLICT OVER REFORM

Things did not, however, go smoothly. Over the course of 1537, it became apparent that getting everyone in Geneva to subscribe to the new articles for the organization of the church would be difficult. Calvin and Farel brought the matter to the attention of the council a number of times.

Things got even worse for Calvin. A man named Pierre Caroli accused Calvin of heresy, meaning that he accused Calvin of teaching things at odds with what was understood to be true Christian tradition. Though found innocent of the charge of Arianism (a heresy that taught that Christ is not fully God), it made plain that there were people in the city willing to see Calvin put to the test, so to speak.

By 1538, the city of Berne, which had helped Geneva gain independence, began to try to enforce a type of uniformity in religious practice. Calvin and Farel wanted to wait until an assembly of reformed ministers met in Zurich to talk through some of these practices, but the Bernese insisted their rules be followed (for example, that only unleavened bread should be used in the Lord's Supper). Furthermore, new elections had been held in Geneva that February, and some of the new political leaders stood against Calvin.

In April 1538, the council demanded that the ministers follow Bernese instructions for celebrating the Lord's Supper, including the use of unleavened bread, for the Easter services. Calvin himself was not opposed to this practice as such, but he thought the issue needed more discussion. He refused to have his hand forced in this manner. Calvin preached the Easter sermon, but he refused to celebrate communion. This flew directly in the face of council orders. He and Farel found themselves, that very week after Easter, exiled from the city.

By this time, the assembly at Zurich had gathered. The ministers there, in fact, sided with Calvin and Farel, though Calvin found himself reprimanded for the way he handled the affair. They thought he should have proceeded more gently with those who disagreed with him. The assembly urged a delegation from Berne to intervene on behalf of Calvin and Farel and have them reinstated as ministers in Geneva. The council, however, refused. Consequently, once again, Calvin took to the road—he was homeless.

AT HOME IN STRASBOURG

After a brief stay in Basel, the Protestant leadership in Strasbourg invited Calvin to come minister to the French refugees in that city. Sitting near the southeastern border of France, Strasbourg took in many who fled the persecution of Francis I.

At first, Calvin refused, thinking that he and Farel should minister together. Several of the evangelical leaders of the Swiss cities, however, did not think Calvin and Farel made a good pair of leaders; perhaps together they made each other too hot-headed at times. Farel accepted a call to minister in the city of Neuchâtel, leaving Calvin to decide what his own fate should be.

By September 1538, Calvin had made his decision and arrived in Strasbourg. There he worked as a pastor to the French while also lecturing on theology. In addition, he practiced law on occasion. He preached or lectured every day, and he gained valuable experience shepherding the French, ministering to them in sickness, overseeing the worship and preaching, and teaching.

There were sad times; people he cared for very much died during this period. He also saw some of his friends from earlier days return to the Catholic Church and renounce the evangelical faith. He once again had to defend his doctrinal position, for Pierre Caroli, who had dogged him in Geneva, reappeared in Strasbourg and brought forward questions about Calvin's orthodoxy.

Despite these troubles, Calvin seemed satisfied with his life in Strasbourg. He was happy enough with his situation there that he applied for and received citizenship, something he had never pursued in Geneva. Moreover, at the urging of his friends and colleagues, Calvin married. Idelette de Bure, a widow with two children, joined Calvin's household in the late summer of 1540.

A THEOLOGIAN AT WORK

This period in Calvin's life also saw the production of some of Calvin's best writing. Within three years, a relatively brief period of time, Calvin revised his *Institutes of the Christian Religion*.

The 1539 edition represented not only an enlargement over the previous edition, but the book was organized in such a way that it looked more like the definitive 1559 edition in terms of its structure. In the 1536 version, Calvin had, somewhat immodestly perhaps, stated in the title that the book embraced "almost the Whole Sum of Piety, and Whatever is Necessary to Know of the Doctrine of Salvation." As a small corrective to that view, the 1539 edition of the *Institutes* added the line, "now corresponding more truly to its title."

The intended audience of the new *Institutes*, as well as its approach to the subject, changed. Calvin now presented his work as something to be read by those who would train in theology in order to properly understand the Word of God, which Calvin understood (at least) to be the Word of Christ as testified to by Scripture. What is more, Calvin came to see the *Institutes*, more than anything else, as a guide for the proper reading of the Bible. The work presented the broad understandings of God, Christ, Holy Spirit, and the church derived from a thorough understanding of the entire Scripture. With that knowledge at hand, one could then approach the individual books of the Bible. Certainly, this new revision of the *Institutes* presented, as Alister McGrath says, "a new clarity of expression and breadth of vision."[12]

In addition, Calvin produced his first biblical commentary (he would eventually write on every book of the New Testament except for Revelation, which he professed not to understand, and on 28 of the 39 books of the Old Testament). The Protestant Reformation has been described by some as a radical appropriation of the Apostle Paul, author of many of the books of the Christian New Testament. Indeed, Martin Luther, considered by many as the first "Protestant," had a conversion experience centered on his reading of Paul's Letter to the Romans, especially with regard to 1:17: "For in it the righteousness of God is revealed through faith for faith: as it is written: 'He who through faith is righteous shall live.'"[13] Luther, and the Protestants who followed after him, took this to mean that one's standing before

God depended upon having faith in God's promises of salvation rather than on good works. This is not to say these Protestants did not believe Christians should do good works; they did. But it is to say they believed one was justified before God by grace (God's free gift of salvation through Christ) through faith first, and then good works were enabled by God as the Christian matured in faith.

Many of the leading Protestant thinkers after Luther wrote commentaries on Romans, since Paul's ideas on grace and faith were so central to the theologies they devised. Calvin was no exception. His first biblical commentary, on Romans, came out in 1540.

Based in part on his humanist training, especially as applied to reading ancient legal texts and commenting upon them, Calvin developed a method of critical interpretation in this commentary that would remain constant throughout the rest of his life. He believed the purpose of a commentary was to explain a biblical passage briefly and clearly. With the burden of theological discussions shifted to the *Institutes*, Calvin did, in fact, produce commentaries that, compared to those of his contemporaries, were relatively brief and clear, usually sticking to the verse or set of verses under consideration without digressing or having to stop and make a long and convoluted theological argument. As T.H.L. Parker has stated, Calvin's "greatest quality as a commentator was his self-disciplined subordination to the text."[14]

In 1541, two other important works appeared, both of which have received some credit for their contribution to the French language. One of these was Calvin's French translation of his *Institutes*. Both the 1536 and 1539 editions were published in Latin, the common language of scholars and churchmen in the sixteenth century. There was an emerging middle class, especially of businessmen and merchants, however, who were literate in their native tongue but not able to read Latin. Some of Calvin's writings were directed toward this group of people. Though Calvin understood his *Institutes* by this time to be a book that could be used in theological studies, this translation makes clear that he never intended to limit his audience to theology students. He cultivated a larger constituency.

The second work represented an early attempt by Calvin to mediate conflicts that had begun to erupt among some of the Protestant leaders. Of all the topics hotly debated in the sixteenth century, none (not even the topic of faith) divided groups as much as the Eucharist. In a way, this makes sense. For well over 1,000 years, the celebration of the meal that commemorated Christ's last supper and the meaning of his death had stood at the center of Christian worship. To change how one viewed that ritual changed how Christians understood themselves, Christ, God, and the church.

A Short Treatise on the Holy Supper of Our Lord Jesus Christ, written first in French and then later translated into Latin, attempted to mediate a conflict that had arisen particularly between the Protestant factions while also stating a positive view of the Supper over against the Catholic Mass. This work showed Calvin at his best: as a mediator who, while holding firm to what he considered essential beliefs, was flexible enough (and charitable enough) to put the best spin on the viewpoints of the two main Protestant factions. He hoped to achieve reconciliation among people who had grown very bitter over this debate, and especially bitter over how their views, they thought, had been misrepresented. He had good intentions; he wanted to help the Protestants reconcile.

Eventually, the subject would make a difficult situation for Calvin, sucking the flexibility and charity out of him. The Protestant movement has been likened to a great ship, and the rock upon which it splintered was competing doctrines of the Eucharist. Calvin himself would become hard in his own opinion, but only after years of attempted mediation.

5

Calvin's Return to Geneva and the Establishment of a Reformed Church: 1541–1549

> For we should understand, that not only has [God]
> called us one day to possess his heavenly inheritance,
> but that by hope he has already in some measure
> installed us in possession; that not only has he
> promised us life, but already transported us into it,
> delivering us from death, when by adopting us as his
> children, he begot us again by immortal seed, namely,
> his word imprinted on our hearts by the Holy Spirit.
>
> —John Calvin,
> Short Treatise on the Holy Supper

I n September 1541, Calvin stood before the congregation of St. Peter's in Geneva, the same place he had refused to celebrate the Lord's Supper on Easter in April 1538. As the service unfolded, Calvin picked up and started preaching where he had left off in 1538.

Even more surprising, perhaps, is that the man who was booted out of town by the council had been wooed back by the council, and when he arrived in 1541, it was with an official city escort. The city had sent a wagon for his family, and they provided a home for the minister and his household.

The period of initial harmony between Calvin and the council was short lived. Conflict erupted from time to time; it simply simmered at others, yet Calvin lived out the rest of his days in Geneva. Why did he come back, and why did he stay? More than anything, perhaps it was a sense of responsibility that settled over him. He had matured in Strasbourg, and he had learned to lead and to organize. He became convinced that God had called him to ministry in Geneva; hence he would serve.

One can see, despite hard feelings over having to leave the city, that Calvin carried with him into exile a sense of obligation for the work he had begun in Geneva. Even before his reluctant return to the city, there appeared a clear sign that he would not simply abandon the city to whatever fate befell it.

REPLY TO CARDINAL SADOLET

Once Farel and Calvin had been exiled, there were those both within and without Geneva that hoped to bring the city back into the Catholic fold. The city's fate appeared unsure.

In the spring of 1539, Cardinal Jacob Sadolet officially wrote to the city council, inviting Geneva back to the Roman church. In an elegant plea, Sadolet asked the Genevans not to turn their backs on the traditions of their fathers for a new religion that was barely decades old. Sadolet not only had the authority of the Catholic Church behind him; he was also known as a man of high character, a scholar, and one who sought to root out abuses in the church.

The council, realizing that it could not answer the letter on its own, sought help. They eventually turned to Calvin. By September 1539, they received Calvin's *Reply*.

"The safety of [a] man," Calvin wrote, "hangs by a thread whose defence turns wholly on this: that he has constantly adhered to the religion handed down to him from his forefathers."[15] Calvin's response to Sadolet served as a defense of the Reformation in Geneva as he refuted Sadolet's letter point by point. He especially emphasized that Protestants, in fact, were not new; they had simply returned to the source of Christianity, Christ and the Scripture that witnessed to him.

The council, certainly, was swayed by the contents of the letter. Never again did there appear to be serious consideration of returning to the Catholic Church.

Again, Calvin exhibited a sense of responsibility in this work he did for Geneva. His own words foreshadow his return to the city, as he wrote to Sadolet, "For though I am for the present relieved of the charge of the Church of Geneva, that circumstance ought not to prevent me from embracing it with paternal affection—God, when he gave it to me in charge, having bound me to be faithful to it forever."[16]

Little did Calvin realize, when he wrote these words, how prophetic they would be.

CALVIN'S RETURN TO GENEVA

Of course, much of what had happened over the course of Calvin's absence related to politics. Parties came into power; parties fell out of favor. Several who had opposed Calvin's work of reform in his first Genevan period were ousted from power in 1539. This explains the willingness of the council to extend a hand to Calvin, asking for his help; essentially, it was not the same council (in terms of the people serving) that had kicked him out.

Indeed, some began to think that it had been a mistake to send Calvin into exile. Certainly, in the interim, his reputation had advanced. What is more, he had learned practical pastoral skills in Strasbourg. Geneva, it turned out, wanted him back. By September 1540, the council had sent representatives to invite Calvin to return.

He shuddered at the thought. In his letters, his rhetoric took flight: He referred to Geneva as "a gulf and a whirlpool which I have already found to be so dangerous and destructive."[17] In another place, he declared, "It would have been far preferable to perish once for all than to be tormented again in that place of torture."[18] After a year of negotiations—Calvin wanted there to be no misunderstanding about how he understood the task of reform—he found himself back in Geneva. At first, he thought he would simply be "on loan" to Geneva for six months, after which time he would return to Strasbourg. There would be, however, no going back.

ORGANIZING A CHURCH

Almost immediately upon his return to Geneva, Calvin began to work on the fundamentals of the church. He penned ordinances for the running of the church (matters of leadership, structure, etc.), and he developed the service of worship. He wrote a catechism in order to instruct the people in the essentials of the type of Christianity he propounded. Finally, he established a fourfold model of church authority and leadership, outlined in the ecclesiastical ordinances.

In the worship service, Calvin encouraged the singing of Psalms. Prayers were said, the Scripture read, and a sermon preached on the text of Scripture. Calvin himself also believed that the Lord's Supper should be celebrated whenever the Word of God was preached, but he never achieved that ideal in the churches of Geneva. So, once per quarter in each of the city churches (which worked out so that communion was celebrated once per month somewhere in Geneva), the minister oversaw communion. Of course, the entire service was conducted in French, the language that the people in Geneva spoke. This was quite a change; everyone had grown up in a church that conducted its service in Latin, which only the educated understood.

Calvin instituted a serial method of Scripture readings and sermons for the churches. Since Reformation leaders valued the Bible as the final source and authority for true Christianity, they thought it best for Scripture to be as fully expounded on and understood as possible. Hence, the sermon "series"; this meant preaching through books of the Bible. Thus, for example, when Calvin started preaching on the book of Job, he started at chapter one verse one, taking a few lines at a time for each sermon, and then he proceeded through the entire book. He ended up preaching 202 sermons on Job.

In his catechism, Calvin taught the fundamentals of faith: the nature of God, the role of Christ, the work of the Holy Spirit. He emphasized the authority of the Bible. He taught, of course, the fundamental Reformation principle: that one is saved by the grace of God alone, through faith. In other words, salvation, in Calvin's thought, is a pure and undeserved gift, something that can only be received through faith and not through good works. Calvin's catechism also taught how one should understand baptism and the Lord's Supper. Both, he said, are ways God imprints on human senses (by sound, touch, sight, taste, smell) what is promised by the Word of God. Word and sacrament reinforce each other.

Finally, Calvin oversaw the development of a fourfold system of ministry. In his plan, a church should have preachers, teachers, elders, and deacons. Preachers preach, administer the sacraments, and provide pastoral care to the people (e.g., visit during times of illness and offer prayers). Teachers educate, promoting true doctrine and expelling errors (although pastors did this as well), lecturing on the Bible, and teaching the catechism. Elders (lay people, not clergy) helped in the work of overseeing the church, especially its discipline. Finally, deacons oversaw the work of helping the poor.

Early in Calvin's tenure, these items—ordinances, worship service, catechism—were presented to the council for its approval. They were accepted (though not without some revision), and

Calvin spent the rest of his life striving to serve the ideals set forth in these documents.

THE COMPANY OF PASTORS

Calvin, of course, was but one man. There were several churches within the city of Geneva proper. Since it was a republic that took in a larger area than just Geneva, however, there were other churches that required pastors: Small towns and rural parishes needed ministers.

THE THREE SOLAS

Much of the writing from the sixteenth century was in Latin; this is especially true of scholarly or academic writing. In Latin, the word *sola* means "alone" or "only." A survey of the major Protestant Reformers makes it clear that there were three solas at the heart of their program for religious reformation.

Sola fide is Latin for "by faith alone." People such as Martin Luther and John Calvin taught that salvation from God is received "by faith alone," apart from the performance of good works. For them, trust in God's promises and God's word of salvation was the key to new life in Christ. Indeed, they believed that humans were incapable of performing the kind of good works that would force God to grant salvation.

Sola gratia means "by grace alone." Because, according to the reformers, human beings could not earn salvation, it had to be given as a free gift from God—that is, one is saved "by grace alone." This concept, for the Reformers, placed the ultimate responsibility for salvation in the hands of God, not human beings. That is why many of them developed doctrines of predestination, the notion that God, apart from human merit, chooses who will be saved. Though they emphasized this belief, it had long been a part of Catholic teaching.

Sola scriptura is translated as "by Scripture alone." For the Reformers, the final and ultimate source of authority was the Bible. Thus, true Christian teaching had to be judged "by Scripture alone" apart from the institutions and traditions of human beings (such as the pope or a council of bishops).

For those who study the Reformation, the three *solas* represent much of what the early Protestants were all about.

Over the course of years, Calvin tried to form a competent group of pastors. Indeed, it became a formal gathering: The Company of Pastors. The company met together for prayer, Bible study, mutual examination of their lives as ministers, and arguments for the correction of errors of thought or life. Calvin held the office of pastor to a high standard.

In a sense, Calvin thought all pastors should be like him. Ideally, he believed a minister should be educated and trained in ancient languages and have the skills to properly interpret the Bible. Calvin expected, moreover, a pastor be adept in the use of language and oratory in order to make the message of the Bible come alive to the congregation. The pastor should be a man called by God, and one whose call is recognized by the congregation and the council. The personality of the pastor should be such that he can be compassionate when needed but forthright in the condemnation of sin when required.

When he first came back to Geneva, the group of pastors there did not meet these expectations. In his zeal for reform, Calvin was harsh at times in his assessment of the ministers, and he did not seem to get along well with the initial group. Over the years, however, through reassignments, outright dismissals, and death, Calvin brought together a group that, eventually, came closer to his ideal. The company became, as a whole, a competent group of ministers.

THE CONSISTORY

The elders, mentioned earlier, together with the Company of Pastors, formed the Consistory. The 12 elders were chosen from among the three city councils, and there were to be representatives from each quarter of the city. The purpose of the Consistory was to enforce church discipline.

Though much has been written about the Consistory over the years, it has been only recently that the records of the Consistory have been made available through the work of a team of scholars. Although stereotyped as an oppressive and intrusive body, willing to punish over the slightest offense, the records show the Consistory to have been something different.

More than anything else, the Consistory sought to create a civil society in which the members of Genevan society could live in peace. Of course, it was assumed all good citizens would attend worship and partake of communion, because these people believed in the possibility of a Christian society. Based on that assumption (which is not, of course, shared by most modern-day Americans), people were therefore called before the Consistory to explain their absence from church.

More than that, however, the Consistory's work appears, based on the records now available, to be that of overseeing good conduct. A variety of cases were brought before the Consistory: those who abused their spouses were admonished; grown sons and daughters who battered their elderly parents were told to behave; parents who severely beat their children found themselves in front of the Consistory. The ideal of Christian society was that all would live in harmony, and the Consistory sought to enable that ideal.

What is more, the Consistory, during Calvin's time, was mostly advisory in its function. The city council never gave it the right to punish; all cases requiring punishment were handed to the civil government. Indeed, not only was the Consistory forbidden to impose civil or criminal penalties on offenders, but it often could not even administer church discipline apart from the sanction of the council. Calvin for years argued that the church and its disciplinary body, the Consistory, should have the right, as a religious punishment, to exclude notorious sinners from the Eucharist. The council fought this idea. The process of excommunication had to go through the civil authorities. For many years, it was the power of persuasion that Calvin and the Consistory exercised rather than direct power over the lives of Genevans.

SOCIAL SERVICES

Pastors preached; teachers taught; elders, along with the pastors, exercised church discipline. The deacons, the final part of Calvin's fourfold model of church organization, played a vital role in developing social services in early modern Geneva.

Calvin believed, and it is clear both from his *Institutes* and his biblical commentaries, that there was a clear mandate for Christians to take care of the poor and needy. Several books have been written on the development of this aspect of the Genevan Reformation, and the model of Geneva inspired other Calvinist churches in other parts of Europe to follow suit. For example, scholars have studied the "bread rolls" of certain seventeenth-century French Calvinist communities, where families who were able took responsibility for providing daily rations of bread to poor families.

Though centuries later some sociologists would argue that in Calvinism there is a spirit that causes capitalism to flourish, there is really nothing in Calvin himself or in Geneva that reflected the notion of a cut-throat capitalism that leaves everyone to fend for himself or herself. Christians were to care for one another, according to Calvin, both spiritually and physically.

DAILY LIFE AS A PASTOR IN GENEVA

Upon his return to Geneva in 1541, Calvin established a work pattern that he would follow until the end of his life in 1564. He preached and lectured on the Bible several times a week; he wrote commentaries on books of the Bible and produced treatises on various theological controversies. He continued to work on his *Institutes of the Christian Religion*, revising and expanding the work that would constitute his chief theological legacy. He engaged in pastoral care; worked with the Consistory and Company of Pastors; and argued with, cajoled, and persuaded the town council on religious matters. He may have also served as town lawyer on occasion.

In addition to these duties, Calvin held dear the value of an education, and he worked toward establishing an educated clergy. This interest would eventually bear fruit in the creation of the Genevan Academy, which has survived to this day in the form of the University of Geneva. Calvin believed that those who preached should be able to draw upon the wellspring of the evangelical faith, the Scripture, and be able to do so in the original languages and knowing something of the context of the times.

Calvin also maintained an international correspondence, advising friends and other reformers how to move forward in the reformed faith and to work for the establishment of congregations: how to structure them and how to provide for worship, preaching, and teaching. In fact, Calvin's connections were so extensive that, it has been said, Calvin was better informed of events throughout Europe than some kings.

CALVIN ATTEMPTS TO MEDIATE A CONFLICT

In addition to mentoring those who had adopted his view of reform in the organization of churches, Calvin played a hand in trying to mediate the differences of belief that had emerged among the Protestants.

No document, perhaps, best illustrates both Calvin's desire to mediate conflict and the divisive nature of the century as the Agreement of Zurich. Calvin worked with the chief pastor of the city of Zurich, Heinrich Bullinger, to develop an understanding of the Eucharist upon which all Protestants could agree.

Calvin had already shown his desire for such an understanding when he wrote his *Short Treatise on the Holy Supper* in 1541. Though the Protestant movement had already begun to splinter in the 1520s, those religious reformers who worked through the civil authorities to bring about change (these are called *magisterial reformers* because they worked through magistrates) fell broadly into two camps: Lutheran (those who closely followed Martin Luther's theology; to learn more about Lutheranism, enter the keywords "lutheranism church" into any Internet search engine and browse the listed websites) and Reformed (representatives of this more diverse movement are Ulrich Zwingli, who was pastor in Zurich before Bullinger; Martin Bucer, the chief pastor of Strasbourg during Calvin's time there; and, a little later, Calvin himself). Calvin's 1541 work represented Calvin's first attempt to mediate between Lutheran and Reformed factions.

By the mid-1540s, however, there were concerns about the relationship between Zurich and Geneva. The result of negotiations on the Eucharist between Calvin and Bullinger was the Agreement of Zurich. Though Calvin and Bullinger certainly did not completely agree on how they understood the Eucharist (Calvin thought the Eucharist a process by which one was put in communion with Christ's true body and blood; Bullinger believed that the primary function of the sacred meal was as a memorial to Christ's sacrifice on the cross), there was common ground that could be a foundation for an agreement, Calvin thought.

The Agreement of Zurich, signed by the parties in 1549, reflected a way of speaking about the Lord's Supper that was flexible in the way it could be read, and this was intended. Each side could hold to their own understanding of the Eucharist while exercising Christian charity in accepting that the other side would not necessarily read the document in the same manner.

The agreement did serve to unite the Swiss Reformed; it did not, however, help sway the Lutherans. Indeed, many Lutherans read the agreement only in the way Bullinger understood it, which, to them, meant a rejection of their view, which was that Christ was present in the Eucharist and was not merely a memorial to Christ's death. For a few years, Calvin continued to try to sway the Lutherans to read the document as something that could possibly express their beliefs. The Lutherans, with their founder having died several years before, believed anything that deviated from Luther's words on the Eucharist was a betrayal of Luther himself.

What began as an attempt at reconciliation among religious parties ended up producing some of the most vicious rhetoric in all the sixteenth century—that between Calvin and the Lutherans. It created a divide that would not be healed.

CALVIN'S HEALTH AND HOME

The emotional and physical strain of Calvin's work began to take its toll. By the end of the decade, Calvin had started to develop ailments that would increasingly make his physical existence painful: His health problems included gout, kidney stones, chronic pulmonary tuberculosis, pleurisy, rheumatism, and migraine headaches.[19] Because Calvin thought his calling came from God, however, throughout the decade he never allowed his pace to lag.

In addition, Calvin's home experienced its share of sadness. He and his wife had at least one son, and maybe more children,[20] but they all died in infancy. Idelette, never really recovering from childbirth, remained sickly for some years, then died in 1549. Calvin continued to care for Idelette's two sons from a previous marriage, but they also preceded Calvin in death. Moreover, one gets the feeling that, though having lived in Geneva for years, Calvin never felt at home. He continued to think of himself as an exile from his homeland. Despite this, he labored on, because he felt God had called on him to do so.

6

Calvin's Geneva: 1550–1564

*I have endeavored, both in my sermons and also in
my writings and commentaries, to preach [God's]
Word purely and chastely, and faithfully to
interpret His sacred Scripture.*

—John Calvin, in his will

O f course, simply recounting the establishment of institutions that would help insure the long-term success of the Reformation in Geneva and the detailing of Calvin's work as pastor makes it sound as if the Reformation in Geneva was an easy process. It was not. Especially in the 1540s and into the 1550s, politicians would criticize Calvin's work, and theologians and teachers would question his theology. Calvin thought of himself as a latter-day David at times (David is traditionally held to have written the Psalms in the Bible). In the language of some of the Psalms of lament, Calvin would ask how long he had to withstand the attacks of evildoers.

Calvin continued to fight for the things he thought the church needed, often in the face of a hostile town council. One of these was the power to enforce excommunication, to exclude wayward Christians from the Lord's Supper as a means of discipline. There continued to be conflict over whether the Consistory could exercise this power on its own, or whether the right to do so lay with the council. Moreover, the council directed, to some extent, how the church would be ordered. Calvin still, after all these years, could not have the Eucharist celebrated as often as he would have liked.

In the first half of the 1550s, Calvin thought a number of times that he would be removed from his post because of his stand against the ruling authorities. The council elections were such that the number of anti-Calvinists grew. As T.H.L. Parker has pointed out, however, these council members did not want Calvin's removal so much as they wanted a "subservient" Calvin.[21] As it turned out, though, not only did they not dismiss Calvin, but the council often either supported him or worked behind the scenes to diffuse difficult situations.

THE CASE OF JEROME BOLSEC

Jerome Bolsec moved to a city near Geneva in 1550 and served as physician to nobility. He had a keen interest in theological matters. He had left the Catholic Church and became a Reformed Protestant. He was most interested in the teachings of Calvin, and he often traveled into Geneva to hear him.

On many points, Bolsec agreed with Calvin's religious teachings. On one matter, however, they disagreed: that of predestination. Calvin had developed a notion of salvation that pointed to God's act of absolute grace as the foundation of redemption. In other words, God chose those who would be saved; moreover, Calvin believed that God actively rejected those who would not be saved. In theological terms, this is called double predestination.

Bolsec disagreed with Calvin on this point, and he publicly argued with Calvin about this doctrine. Calvin brought heresy charges against Bolsec. The city council wrote other Reformed churches and theologians for their opinions. Some sided with Calvin; others did not.

This presented a dilemma for the council. If they found in favor of Bolsec, it would be as if they were saying that Calvin taught false doctrine; and Calvin was, after all, employed by the council itself to teach and interpret the Bible. It would be as if the council were condemning itself. Unfortunately, this mindset that one could only be absolutely right or absolutely wrong in matters of essential doctrine characterized much sixteenth-century thinking.

Bolsec thus found himself banished for life from the city of Geneva. Though he wandered from place to place in Switzerland for a time, he eventually found his way back to France, where he joined himself once again to the Catholic Church.

Although Calvin may have won this battle with the express backing of the town council, this may be a case of a victory won too dearly. Bolsec later wrote a biography of Calvin that has helped to cast Calvin, historically, as a villain—the tyrant of Geneva.

THE CASE OF PHILIBERT BERTHELIER

Though personalities are involved in this case, they are representative of larger problems in Geneva. Philibert Berthelier

JOHN CALVIN

Map of the Holy Roman Empire during Calvin's time.

John Calvin, depicted here as a young man, trained to be a lawyer in his youth. It was while studying law in Orléans and Bourges that Calvin became influenced by humanism. After he graduated with his law degree, Calvin had hopes of becoming a humanist scholar.

After French troops forcibly moved the papacy to this fortress in French-controlled Avignon in 1309, other countries tried to restore the papacy to Rome. This crisis, now known as the Great Schism, resulted in the fracturing of the Catholic Church between two popes—one in Avignon and one in Rome.

King Francis I of France was born in 1494 and died in 1547. He ascended the throne in 1515, ruling for much of John Calvin's life. Francis had the daunting task of leading the Catholic country during the rocky early years of the Protestant Reformation.

Martin Luther was a German monk who gained fame after he penned his "Ninety-Five Theses" in 1517. The document, which was intended only to incite debate and, hopefully, changes in the Catholic Church, led to the major crisis known as the Protestant Reformation. Luther's ideas, particularly those on the salvation of the soul, greatly influenced Calvin.

This monument in Geneva, where Calvin spent a great deal of his life writing, preaching, and establishing Protestant churches, honors key figures in the Protestant Reformation. Those pictured are, from left to right: William Farel, who worked closely with Calvin in Geneva during his first period there; John Calvin; Theodore Beza, who assisted Calvin and then carried on his work as a Protestant leader in Geneva; and John Knox, who is credited with bringing Protestantism to Scotland.

Michael Servetus was known as a religious heretic throughout Europe for denying the concept of the trinity. He escaped from prison in one city and traveled to Geneva, where Calvin filed heresy charges against him. After a council found Servetus guilty and sentenced him to death, Calvin attempted to win a more humane execution for Servetus—beheading—but it was in vain: on October 27, 1553, Servetus was burned at the stake.

John Calvin speaks at the Council of Geneva in 1549.
Relations were often tense between Calvin and the council.

This oil painting by the artist Titian depicts the Last Supper of Christ, during which Jesus offered the apostles bread and wine, saying they were his "body and blood." This event is re-enacted in Christian church services and became a matter of some debate between Lutheran and Reformed Protestants during Calvin's time in Geneva (as well as between Protestants and Catholics). The point of contention between the Lutherans and Calvin revolved around the question concerning how Christ was present to those who participated in the meal. The notion that Christ is present in the celebration of the Eucharist was firmly established in Christian belief by the time of Calvin.

had been excommunicated by the Consistory. As the quarterly celebration of the Lord's Supper approached in September 1553, however, he directly requested that the council reinstate him to full communion with the church so that he might take the Eucharist. The council did so, although they asked Berthelier not to partake of the Lord's Supper that particular Sunday.

On the communion Sunday in September 1553, Calvin directly forbade those excommunicated by the Consistory from partaking of the Eucharist. He stated in the strongest terms that those who had not shown true repentance to the Consistory could not be reinstated by the council. He expected to be fired for such a stance, and that afternoon he preached a farewell sermon.

Calvin was not, however, forced from the pulpit by the council. Instead, they chose to study the problem, examining the ecclesiastical ordinances of 1541. Here again, the council ended up supporting Calvin, deciding that the council should not nullify excommunication when the person who had been excommunicated showed no sign of repentance before the Consistory.

The question dragged on, however, for the next two years. At points, the council claimed the right to decide excommunication itself. At other times, it softened its stance. New elections in 1555 finally pushed the matter in the Consistory's favor.

The Berthelier case, however, is representative of a larger conflict taking place in Geneva. The seeming hostility between Calvin and the council, between Calvin and the city of Geneva, has been characterized in a variety of ways. From Calvin's point of view, it was a matter of taking seriously the Bible's ethical injunctions, and he labeled those who were frustrated under his religious leadership as immoral. Yet, it is clear the council also had interest in maintaining moral standards within the city. From the point of view of some of Calvin's opponents, the problem was that Calvin wanted to rule the city, and this image is what helped contribute to the notion that Calvin was a theocrat, that is, was a religious leader who ruled with an iron fist over society. This stereotype, however, cannot be upheld by the historical evidence any more than Calvin's insistence that it was simply the general immorality of Genevans that was the point of conflict.

William Naphy, a professor at the University of Aberdeen, has suggested that, based on the historical evidence of social changes in Geneva, the problem centered on the shift in demographics. Native Genevans frequently "protested against the increasing size and influence of the French refugee community."[22] Berthelier was connected to the native families of Geneva who had helped Geneva break free of the rule of Savoy. Certain people in Geneva grew to resent the influence of foreign ministers such as Calvin. Moreover, because of the influx of French refugees (caused by religious persecution)—many of whom became strong supporters of Calvin—the political balance began to shift away from the old Geneva families. Thus, as much as a religious problem, Berthelier's stance against Calvin was a political statement against the rule of foreigners.

These tensions continued to show up in, of all places, conflicts over the naming of children at the time of baptism. Calvin favored biblical names for children, and so he rejected many of the traditional names (often the names of Catholic saints) that parents wanted to give their children. Although this issue arose in the 1540s, it had reached crisis proportions by 1550. Riots broke out. Arrests were made. This problem that Calvin perhaps saw blindly as a religious one makes evident the same fear noted earlier: "Many Genevans saw this baptismal policy as an attempt to force a foreign practice on them."[23] This inflamed anti-Calvin and anti-French sentiment. And yet, as close as dismissal seemed at times for Calvin, the council never took such drastic action. It would not be long before the possibility of such action disappeared.

THE EXECUTION OF SERVETUS

Perhaps nothing is more ironic, in a way, in the study of Calvin than the affair of Michael Servetus. In his own century, the capture, trial, and execution of Servetus won for Calvin international acclaim. In later centuries, the affair has been used to paint Calvin as a depraved and despicable man, one whose theology naturally led to such abominable behavior as the execution of a man over a simple difference of opinion. In reality, however, Calvin acted in a way consistent with the behavior of most people of the sixteenth century. People were, in fact, executed by civil governments for religious heresy in part, from the governmental perspective, to maintain civil order.

Zurich saw multiple executions related to what were considered baptismal heresies; the government of France routinely burned heretics; in Spain, there was the Inquisition. Martin Luther wrote a tract ("Against the Thieving and Murderous Hordes of Peasants") that encouraged the princes to slay those

THE LIFE OF MICHAEL SERVETUS

Probably born about the same time as John Calvin (around 1509), Michael Servetus well represented what came to be known as the "Renaissance man." He had a well-rounded education, and he ably participated in several realms of scholarly inquiry. For example, he wrote a book on the ancient geographer Ptolemy, and the book had enough influence that it is still included in histories of geography. He, like so many Renaissance figures (such as Leonardo da Vinci), had an interest in science. He had studied human anatomy, and his work anticipated the work of William Harvey, who published his famous theories in 1628 on the circulation of the blood.

It is in the area of religion, however, that Servetus is most remembered. He advanced a view of God that denied the traditional Christian doctrine of the Trinity. He taught, instead, that God expressed himself through a variety of names, and each manifestation under a particular name was meant to teach a certain message about God. Jesus and the Holy Spirit were two of the many names by which the one God could be known.

Servetus fully engaged the humanist spirit of the time. With the motto of the humanists, "Back to the Sources," as his principle, he sought to show how his views on God and Christ reconstructed the beliefs of earliest Christianity.

Though executed as a heretic in his own time in Calvin's Geneva, Servetus's thought was influential in the eventual development of Unitarianism, the belief that there is only one God and that the doctrine of the Trinity is indefensible.

who rebelled against the established order. England, under Queen Elizabeth I, witnessed the execution of hundreds of religious dissenters. It is interesting that Calvin seems to bear the brunt of contemporary objections to the execution of religious dissenters. This has happened despite the fact that Servetus represents the sole execution for religious causes in Geneva during Calvin's time there. Certainly, killing someone for a difference in religious opinion should not be sanctioned, yet it happened routinely in the sixteenth century. What is extraordinary is that it happened only once in Calvin's Geneva.

In 1553, Michael Servetus came through Geneva. He was known throughout Europe as an infamous heretic. He was best known as an anti-trinitarian; that is, he did not believe the traditional Christian doctrine that God is one God, yet also three: Father, Son, and Holy Spirit. He had already been arrested in another city, but he escaped; his sentence there was to be executed by fire.

Calvin recognized Servetus while he was in Geneva and filed heresy charges against him, and Servetus was arrested in mid-August. It is important to note, however, that this trial took place under the guidance of the city council because, as Alister McGrath has pointed out so ably, the council's "persecution of Servetus . . . was intended to demonstrate their impeccable orthodoxy, as a prelude to undermining Calvin's religious authority within the city. The Consistory . . . was bypassed altogether by the council in its efforts to marginalize Calvin from the affair." [24]

The council did call Calvin in as chief theological expert. Servetus found himself, for the second time, condemned to death for his theological beliefs. Calvin attempted to have the more humane method of execution—beheading—applied to Servetus, but the city council insisted instead that Servetus be slowly burned to death.

Once again, it should be noted how differently this event was viewed in the sixteenth century. Vienna had requested Servetus's extradition so that he could be put to death in that city.

Congratulations came in from the surrounding Swiss towns and from other cities throughout the Holy Roman Empire. The event enhanced Calvin's international reputation, and it helped to further establish him as one of the chief leaders of the Protestant movement.

GENEVA: A PRO-CALVIN TOWN

Despite the Servetus affair, and perhaps the inadvertent elevation of Calvin's reputation, there were those who still hoped to see Calvin removed. Philibert Berthelier once again brought his petition to be reinstated into the communion of the church in November 1553, and this time the council, after debate, decided that the Consistory, on its own, did not have the power to exclude the unrepentant from communion. Still, the debate continued.

Finally, in 1555, matters took a turn in Calvin's favor. In January, after consultation with some of the other Swiss cities, the council decided once again that the ecclesiastical ordinances of 1541 should be followed, and the power of excommunication should be in the hands of the Consistory (which, after all, had representatives from the council sitting upon it). Then the February 1555 elections saw the overwhelming defeat of the anti-Calvinist party. Later, in the spring, a large number of French refugees were given citizenship. Some of the old guard—the "Geneva for Genevans" sort of group—objected to this action, and when their complaints fell on deaf ears, they began threatening to take power back. Though there was never really a rebellion as such, some of the ringleaders had caused enough of a stir that some people were arrested; others fled. From this point forward, Calvin no longer had to deal with an openly hostile council. The majority of the council and the leaders within the council were solidly in Calvin's camp.

CALVIN'S WORK COMPLETED

In this new atmosphere, Calvin simply continued his work as a reformer. He preached, taught, and wrote. The 1550s saw two major editions of the *Institutes* published. One appeared in 1550, but it was the 1559 edition, the final Latin edition, that would serve as the one book upon which so much of Calvin's historical reputation would rest.

Two other events—one of a perhaps more private nature, one of a much more public nature—took place in 1559. For one whose identity is so connected to a city, it is surprising that Calvin did not become a citizen of Geneva until 1559, only five years before his death. Thus, Calvin served the city of Geneva without citizen status for approximately 19 of his 24 years in residence.

On a more public scale, 1559 finally saw the opening of the Genevan Academy. As early as 1541, Calvin encouraged the council to fund an educational system. Calvin believed very strongly that the church needed educated people to provide leadership. Finally, land was obtained and a building started in 1558. Though work would continue for some years on the physical structure, the opening ceremonies were held in July 1559 in St. Peter's Church.

Calvin sought the best teachers he could get for his school. The person appointed to head the academy was a New Testament scholar named Theodore Beza, a man who would eventually succeed Calvin as chief pastor of the city of Geneva (to learn more about Calvin's successor, enter the keywords "Theodore Beza Geneva" into any Internet search engine and browse the listed websites). This institution, over the years, would eventually be transformed into what is known today as the University of Geneva. Students came from all over Europe to study there, and this academy would continue for a very long time as one of the primary training grounds for ministers in the Reformed faith. This institution served, along with the *Institutes*, as the foundation for the continuation and development of Calvin's theological program.

CALVIN'S DEATH

John Calvin died on May 27, 1564. He had not quite reached his fifty-fifth birthday. He had been in ill health for years. At one point, he could not walk to St. Peter's to preach, so people carried him. By February 1564, however, he could no longer preach at all. By April, he knew death was near, and at the end of the month he gave his last will and address to the magistrates and ministers of Geneva.

He made arrangements for the distribution of his very modest estate. He reflected on his ministry in Geneva. On the one hand, Calvin seems harsh on the Genevans. He spoke at length of their immorality and opposition to the gospel. On the other hand, he also acknowledged his own shortcomings, his impatience, and his lack of tact on numerous occasions.

In the end, however, Calvin threw himself and his ministry upon God's grace, believing that "God is the Father of mercy [and] will show himself such a Father to me, who acknowledge myself to be a miserable sinner."[25] Summarizing his life's work, he said simply, "I have endeavored, both in my sermons and also in my writings and commentaries, to preach [God's] Word purely and chastely, and faithfully to interpret His sacred Scripture."[26]

At his death, Calvin was buried in Geneva in an unmarked grave in accordance with his wishes. Its place was never disclosed. In a sense, then, it was as if his body at death simply disappeared from Geneva—it was nowhere to be found. Yet his spirit—through the influence of the institutions he helped to build, the books he wrote, the students he taught—not only filled Geneva but also inspired Reformed Christians throughout Europe and eventually the world.

7

Calvin and the Word of God

. . . [I]t is faith that must cleanse us. . . . If men enjoin spiritual laws upon us, we need not observe them, being assured that such obedience cannot please God, for in so doing, we set up rulers to govern us, making them equal with God, who reserveth all power to Himself. Thus, the government of the soul must be kept safe and sound in the hands of God.

—John Calvin, sermon,
"The Word Our Only Rule"

"To preach [God's] Word purely and chastely" is how Calvin understood the work of Christian ministry. Though it is a short phrase—God's Word—it is at the heart of Calvin's understanding of God and how God is revealed and reconciled to humanity. It is also a complicated phrase that is weighted with several interlocking meanings.

Calvin believed human beings could never understand God as God; human beings could only grasp God insofar as God chose to reveal himself. But because Calvin believed God to be a "good Father," to use one of his favorite metaphors, he also believed God engaged in a process of accommodation in order to commune and communicate with his children.

The word accommodation simply means to make suitable. Calvin thought that God had taken a number of steps to make himself and his purpose suitable for human understanding. Martin Luther once said that God engaged in baby talk in order to speak to humanity. Calvin's thoughts are along the same line, though they operate on a much larger scale than just speech. The rest of this chapter will detail the variety of ways Calvin thought God accommodated himself in order to reveal his good will and purpose to his children. All of these accommodations can be understood at some level as "God's Word."

THE WORD MADE FLESH: JESUS CHRIST

Following traditional Christian teaching, John Calvin believed that Jesus was the savior. He thought humanity as a race had essentially "gone bad" by rebelling against God. Jesus served as the mediator between God and humanity, and through his death on a cross, Jesus atoned for sin. He set straight the cosmic scales of justice, and he placed the Christian into proper relationship with God.

Also following traditional Christian teaching, Calvin believed that Jesus was not only human but also divine, part of the Trinity of Father, Son, and Holy Spirit. Thus, the divine nature in Jesus existed from eternity and was properly part of God.

In the beginning of the New Testament Gospel of John, this divine aspect of Jesus is described as the "word": "In the beginning was the word, and the word was with God, and the word was God. This one, he was in the beginning with God." A few verses later, the Gospel of John states, "And the word became flesh, and dwelt among us." This is the basis of the Christian teaching about incarnation—a word that comes from Latin that literally means "enfleshed." Thus, at the birth of Jesus, the divine Word of God took on a body.

In its most fundamental sense for Calvin, the Word of God meant Jesus Christ. Thus, whenever he spoke of preaching the Word of God, at the heart of that Word was the person of Jesus Christ.

It is here that we can see clearly the notion of accommodation at work in Calvin. Though he accepted the traditional teachings of the church of Christ as savior and Christ as the word made flesh, his way of explaining how the salvation process works reflects his concern that God works to make himself "suitable" for human understanding.

In one of his sermons, Calvin states bluntly that Christ is mediator between God and humanity insomuch as Christ is human. "We cannot know Jesus Christ to be a mediator between God and man," Calvin proclaimed, "unless we behold him as man."[27] That does not mean the divine nature is unimportant, but it is to say that the way Christians receive the gift of salvation from God comes through Christ's humanity. This is the way Calvin explains it in his *Commentary on John.*

He says that righteousness, that which makes human beings fit to be in communion with God, properly resides in God alone. Because the divine part of Christ is part of God, belonging to the Holy Trinity, however, that righteousness also properly belongs to the Son, Christ. That righteousness is then transferred from the divine person of Christ to the human person of the incarnated Christ Jesus. Then it is through Jesus's humanity that the righteousness of God is bestowed upon Christians in their humanity. In other words, Calvin said, "His [Christ's] flesh is a channel to pour out to us the life which resides intrinsically . . . in His divinity."[28]

It is Christ's life in the body (the incarnation) that Christ speaks, ministers, teaches, heals, dies, and is resurrected. Thus, for Calvin, it is through communion with the human Christ, through Christ's spirit, through Christ's words, but also through Christ's body (this shall be discussed at greater length later) that Christians obtain the benefits of his grace, his gift of salvation.

Though Calvin has sometimes been painted as one who had a very somber view of God, one that makes God seem far removed from humanity because of God's great majesty, his way of talking about Christ was his method to, in a sense, "humanize" God, which is what the incarnation was really all about in Calvin's mind. Thus, in reading Calvin, for all his intellectual abilities, one comes across a very tender view of Christ and the Christian's relationship to Christ. It is this Christ that is the Word of God accommodated to fit human weakness, so that humanity may understand God's love.

THE WRITTEN WORD: THE HOLY SCRIPTURE

Calvin's first job in Geneva, and one he continued through all his years in that city, was as a Reader of Holy Scripture, meaning that he taught about the Bible. Calvin believed that the Bible was a further accommodation by God to human weakness. It made clear God's will, and it prophesied the coming of Christ and then bore witness to his life, ministry, death, and resurrection.

The Bible served to make clear what sinful nature had blurred. For example, Calvin believed that the universe itself was enough to proclaim God's existence and God's goodness. The will of God, as it were, was written large across the skies, in the sun and moon and stars and in the earth. Human beings, however, because of sin, could not read rightly the signs set before them in the physical world. According to Calvin, Scripture worked as "spectacles"—eye glasses that brought the created order into focus so that Christians could see God's goodness in God's creation.

Calvin also thought that embedded in each human being was a conscience—a natural ability to tell right from wrong. Again, because of sin, however, this ability had been warped. Therefore, God accommodated to human weakness, and in the Bible spelled out what should be plain in each person's heart: Do not lie; do not steal; do not murder. In other words, the moral code of the Ten Commandments found in the Old Testament and the reinforcement of that morality in the New Testament in the Sermon on the Mount were gifts of God, written in plain language to help those who had lost the right use of conscience.

At the heart of the Scripture for Calvin, however, was Jesus Christ. He believed that Christ, because as divine he was eternal, could be read about in the Old Testament (before his being born on earth). Not only did prophets foretell his coming, according to Calvin; he also believed that there were "types" of Christ in the Old Testament that outlined what the Christ-to-be-born would be like.

The New Testament, of course, contained the witness to Christ: the words he spoke, the life he lived, and the cross he bore. The gospels presented the life of Jesus; other books, such as the letters of the Apostle Paul, presented the true teachings about the meaning of Jesus's life.

Whereas Christ, then, was the living Word, the Bible was the written Word, accommodated to humanity's need and weakness. It served as a sure guide to understanding the Word made flesh, Jesus Christ. Hence, Calvin believed the study of the Bible, in its original languages (mostly Hebrew and Greek), to be essential for the health of the Christian church. He thought the task of the interpreter of Scripture—someone like himself— was to lay bare the mind of the author. Of course, in an immediate sense, that meant laying bare the mind of Moses, whom Calvin understood to have written Genesis; or of Paul, who wrote so many letters; or of one of the Gospel writers. In a deeper sense, however, Calvin believed he was laying bare the mind of God, the ultimate author of Scripture, at least in the accommodated way God made himself known through Christ in Scripture.

It is interesting to note, however, that Calvin did not set the Bible up as a thing to be worshiped unto itself; he believed the Bible to be an instrument used by God for the purpose of presenting Christ. The real value of the Bible for Calvin lay in the way in which the Holy Spirit—the Spirit that Christians traditionally believe flows from God and Christ—could breathe life into the Scripture and make of it a living thing that could unite the Christian to Christ and make Christ present and real.

Calvin certainly believed that the Bible stood as the foundation of truth about Christ. He joined many early Protestants in their cry of "Scripture Alone!" when it came to seeing the Bible as the only source of authority for true Christian faith and worship. In order for that truth to make a life-changing difference, however, one would have to be illumined by the flame of the Holy Spirit, and the Spirit works, through the words of Scripture, to unite the Christian with Christ. As one scholar has noted when speaking of Calvin's view of Scripture, "Scripture comes alive in fellowship with Christ."[29]

THE SPOKEN WORD: CHRIST MADE PRESENT BY PREACHING

John Calvin held to an exalted view of preaching. Whereas he held the Scripture in the highest esteem and valued its private and public study, he especially emphasized the preached Word of God, based on Scripture. At one point, in his commentary on Paul's Letter to the Romans, Calvin states, "The Word . . . is required for a true knowledge of God. But it is the preached Word alone which Paul has described, for this is the normal mode which the Lord has appointed for imparting His Word."[30]

Indeed, the act of preaching was so important to Calvin because he saw it as one of the primary ways in which God had chosen to be present. Christ, Calvin thought, practically stood among the congregation when preachers purely spoke the Word of God. "If the Gospel be not preached," Calvin proclaimed, "Jesus Christ is, as it were, buried." [31] In another place, Calvin boldly stated, "Jesus Christ shows himself openly to those who have the eyes of faith to look upon Him, when the gospel is preached." [32] Of course, Calvin believed God had to will this to take place, and the Holy Spirit had to effect the presence. God was in charge, not humans. Given that caveat, however, Calvin very much believed that God did act to present Christ in preaching.

In a sense, preaching represented a type of "time machine" for Calvin. The written Word, the Bible, recounted events from hundreds of years before: important events, such as the death

PREACHING GOD'S WORD

Some estimates place the number of sermons given by Calvin at more than 4,000. He believed passionately that the sermon, based on Scripture, served as God's Word to the congregation.

Because he believed Scripture—because connected to Christ—to be the living Word of God, he understood it to be the preacher's task to make the Scripture come alive. He always thought that, once the best techniques were applied to the text of Scripture in order to understand its author's mind, the lessons of that text should be brought into contemporary life. In other words, he believed that Scripture had to do as much with the present as with the past.

Calvin always wanted the preaching of Scripture to have an effect, not just on the person's head, but also on the heart. The best way to do that, according to Calvin, was to pick the right expression, the appropriate figure of speech, to convey the significance of the Word of God. He preached in the familiar style, using common and everyday expressions and metaphors to explore the meaning of Scripture. Couched in such language, he thought, the Word could more easily penetrate the heart of the believer.

At its best and most effective, Calvin believed preaching lifted the congregation into the very presence of God. No wonder, then, that he devoted so much time to it.

of Jesus on the cross. The spoken Word, preaching, bridges the time span, taking the events of the Bible and, through the inspiration of the Holy Spirit, bringing them to life in the present. It is one thing, according to Calvin, to believe that Christ once died. It is another to realize, through the preached Word, that the death of Christ makes a difference in the present; whereas the Scripture testifies to a Christ who was raised from the dead, the sermon preaches Christ raised now and living among his people. Indeed, as Brian Gerrish has stated, "The idea of Christ's living presence, effected through the Word of God, is the heart of Calvin's gospel."[33]

No wonder Calvin placed so much emphasis on preaching and learning to preach well. He thought one should be trained in ancient languages and history, in the use of language and rhetoric, so that the living Word about which the written Word speaks might be placed before Christians to learn from, live with, and love.

THE VISIBLE WORD: THE EUCHARIST AND THE PRESENCE OF CHRIST

Calvin believed that, just as Christ is offered in the preached Word, so Christ is also presented to believers in the Eucharist. In fact, referring to both baptism and the Eucharist (the two sacraments of Reformed Christianity), Calvin taught that the promises God offers are seen most clearly in the sacraments. The reason, Calvin explained, is that since human beings learn and know things through their senses, a sacrament like the Eucharist engages all of a Christian's senses: One sees the bread and wine, touches the elements, smells the food, and tastes it; these senses, in turn, reinforce what is heard during the service about God's promises.

What God promises is forgiveness of sin through the mediation of Christ, and Calvin thought that the mediation of Christ involved a real communion with him; in fact, more than simply communion, Calvin wrote that between Christ and the Christian there is a real union by which the benefits of Christ—the living

Word—are shared with the Christian. Calvin meant not just a union with Christ's spirit, but also Christ's body, because it is the human person of Christ that is the mediator between God and humanity.

Calvin tried for years to fully explain how he thought Christ was truly present in the Eucharist. He did not believe like the Catholics, who thought that the bread and wine became the body and blood of Christ; he did not think like the Lutherans, who believed that, while the bread and wine remained intact, the body and blood of Christ were added to these things; and he did not believe like the Zwinglians, who thought the bread and wine simply represented Christ's body and blood, so that Christ was not present bodily in the act of the Eucharist.

If Calvin did not believe these things, what did he believe? He himself was always the first person to say he did not fully understand how the Christian could commune with Christ's body and blood, but he did forcefully state that he experienced such a communion. Furthermore, he thought that such union with Christ was essential to salvation. He ended up teaching that, in the act of the Eucharist, through the instruments of bread and wine, the Christian's spirit was lifted into the divine realm, there to commune with the true, full Christ, body and blood. Participation in the Eucharist, having the senses flooded with the signs of bread and wine being taken into and united to the body of the believer, served as a visible Word by which the Christian was united to the living Word Christ. And it is clear that such talk was not simply metaphorical for Calvin.

Indeed, one of Calvin's most passionate defenses of his notion of union with Christ through the instrument of the Eucharist is his commentary on the New Testament book of Ephesians, chapter 5, which is about a husband and a wife. Calvin takes this type of union as the model for the closeness of the Christian's union with Christ.

Calvin could never fully explain how such a union could take place. Still, he held strongly to this position, in the end simply proclaiming, "I am overwhelmed by the depth of this mystery."[34]

Indeed, a sense of awe sat at the heart of Calvin's religious experience and thought. The gracious Word of God in all its senses, one accommodation after another to human weakness, if truly believed and grasped, could finally draw forth only one appropriate response: utter thankfulness in light of God's unfathomable goodness. Indeed, as one scholar has said, "The theme of grace and gratitude . . . lies at the heart of Calvin's entire theology."[35]

8

Calvin's Theology

*We have been redeemed by Christ at so great a price . . .
so . . . we should not enslave ourselves to the wicked
desires of men much less be subject to their impiety.*

—John Calvin,
Institutes of the Christian Religion

John Calvin is considered one of the greatest theologians of the Protestant tradition, oftentimes seen, along with Martin Luther, as one of the fundamental thinkers of Protestantism. In a broader view, he is often portrayed as one of the most influential theologians of the Western Christian tradition. In histories of Christian theology, he often holds a prominent place. Catholics as well as Protestants write now on Calvin's theology. Courses on Calvin's thought are offered in Catholic universities. Of course, not everyone agrees with the things Calvin believed (Protestants or Catholics), but there is no getting away from the fact that, since his lifetime, Calvin has been one of the major theological voices in Western Christianity.

A theologian is one who attempts to present a coherent and compelling understanding of God and God's relationship to the world. Calvin wrote many books that present his view on these matters. Some were biblical commentaries; others were treatises on particular problems, such as the Eucharist. His letters contain much theology.

Historically, however, Calvin's primary influence has come through his *Institutes of the Christian Religion*. Indeed, it was once said and widely accepted that "The whole of Calvinism is in the *Institutes*."[36] Whereas those in Calvin studies today generally believe that more than the *Institutes* must be read to understand Calvin himself, it is still true that, for most of history, Calvin has been associated with the *Institutes*. Indeed, even today, the *Institutes* remain foundational (though not exclusively so) for a study of Calvin's theology. Because Calvin himself claimed that the work contained "almost the whole sum of piety and whatever it is necessary to know in the doctrine of salvation," it serves as a good introduction to Calvin's religious thought.

THE STRUCTURE OF THE *INSTITUTES*

Whereas the earliest edition of the *Institutes* (1536) contained only six chapters, the final Latin edition (1559) used a different system of organization. The work was divided into four books; each book was divided into chapters; each chapter had numbered sections. Because of its systematic arrangement, it is common now when citing the *Institutes* to do so in that order: book number, chapter, and section number. Thus, when reading a book about Calvin that refers to his *Institutes*, this system, rather than citing page numbers, is used, and this works whether the edition being cited is in Latin, English, or some other language. Thus, for example, when Calvin states that "Nearly all the wisdom we possess, that is to say, true and sound wisdom, consists of two parts: the knowledge of God and of ourselves," it is cited this way: *Institutes* 1.1.1. This means that the sentence is found in book one, chapter one, section one.

Before chapter one, however, one finds two addresses: one to the reader and one to King Francis I. In speaking to the reader, Calvin testifies that the order of the topics was important to him; he says he was never satisfied until this latest edition with the arrangement of themes. This says something important about the way Calvin thought about theology: the order of topics, and their relationship to one another, is important. To properly understand true doctrine, Calvin thought, one had to grasp its parts in the correct order. For example, one could not appropriately grasp the meaning of the church unless one had first correctly understood the work of Christ. Arrangement mattered.

Also important is Calvin's stated purpose: to teach candidates in theology to so grasp the Christian religion that they can then properly understand and interpret the Bible. The *Institutes* serve as the doctrinal foundation for his biblical commentaries.

Even though King Francis I had died more than a decade before 1559, Calvin kept his letter to him in his *Institutes*. Though a different ruler sat upon the throne, Calvin believed the principles articulated in his original dedicatory letter still applied: that the reform movement represented true Christianity, a return to the old faith of the Apostles; that charges of immorality against the reformers were false; that the king should give to the reformers a fair hearing; and, finally, that, fair hearing or not, God would vindicate the innocent.

THE FOUR BOOKS

Calvin divided his 1559 *Institutes* into four books. The first deals with God as creator, the second with God as redeemer, the third with the way the grace of Christ is received, and the fourth has to do with external aids by which God joins the Christian to Christ.

Book One: The Knowledge of God the Creator

Calvin believed that the knowledge of God and the knowledge of self are interrelated. To truly know God is to know God's greatness; to really understand self, humans must recognize their shortcomings and failings. Compared to God, humanity is nothing.

Though related, Calvin thought that "the order of right teaching requires" that one first turn toward the knowledge of God.[37] Here, Calvin emphasized that he meant, in a sense, the *practical* knowledge of God. He was less interested in philosophical questions about God and God's essence and much more interested in a knowledge that flows from piety, or knowledge based in love and reverence for God. This is an attitude that places trust in God and seeks to worship God. The pious approach to the knowledge of God is one that simply receives what God offers, and God, Calvin believed, offered the knowledge of himself that was necessary for salvation. To seek beyond this knowledge, Calvin thought, represented vain speculation.

God implanted knowledge of himself into the minds of all human beings. Everyone, according to Calvin, has some sense of God, yet that knowledge has been corrupted. People turn away from God; some engage in superstition; others build idols; hypocrites look to God only when they are in trouble and want something. Indeed, humans "entangle themselves in such a huge mass of errors that blind wickedness stifles and finally extinguishes those sparks which once flashed forth to show them God's glory."[38]

Furthermore, Calvin taught that the knowledge of God can be seen in the work of God's creation, including the creation of

humankind. Indeed, as Calvin wrote, "We must therefore admit in God's individual works but especially in them as a whole that God's powers are actually represented as in a painting."[39] Because true knowledge of God is the goal of what Calvin called the blessed life, the display of this knowledge through-out the created order renders inexcusable humans' lack of knowledge. Calvin felt that humans truly lacked knowledge of God, as evident in a world full of false worship, superstition, and vain speculation.

In accommodation to human weakness and failing, then, God created an aid for humanity—the Scripture. Here is where one finds Calvin's famous metaphor of the Bible as "spectacles," that is, as eyeglasses by which the universe might be read rightly.[40] Thus, God as creator might be known.

As the Word of God, Calvin believed that Scripture had its authority directly from God. This means that the church, far from being the judge of Scripture, is itself always to be grounded in and judged by the Scripture.

True Christians will heed the Bible, for the Holy Spirit, Calvin taught, seals the truth of Scripture upon the hearts of all believers. Christians know the Bible to be true, and its doctrines to be trustworthy, because the Holy Spirit of God teaches them so. Furthermore, although there are many credible proofs, according to Calvin, of the reliability of Scripture, in the end it is the testimony of the Holy Spirit that matters most.

From Scripture, then, one learns about the one true God who is to be worshiped. Therefore, there is no reason to bow down before false idols. As part of defining the true God, Calvin affirmed the traditional Christian belief in the Trinity: the notion that God is one God in three persons, historically identified as God the Father, God the Son, and God the Holy Spirit, all sharing, however, the same essence.

The *Institutes* then move to a discussion of human nature. Calvin believed that humans were created pure by God, each person being composed of a body and a soul. Within the soul resides the image of God in each and every human being. That

image has been tarnished, however, and can only be truly seen by looking at a person's redemptive state in Christ.

The parts of the human soul are understanding (the intellect) and the will (the faculty by which choices are made). Because of the will, humans had the ability to choose eternal life, yet, this did not happen. Calvin believed that there was a "Fall," a time when the first man and woman, Adam and Eve, turned away from God. Thus, humans have the stain of original sin, which has affected and damaged the will. Calvin will have more to say of this later on in his book.

Finally, in dealing with the notion of God the Creator, Calvin set forth the doctrine of providence: the idea that God continues to oversee the entirety of creation as well as individual lives. Calvin believed that nothing that happened in the world occurred apart from God's will; although God's purpose in events might be hidden, the Christian could take comfort in the belief that God supervises creation. God uses the instruments of his will, the godly and the godless alike, to accomplish his purposes. For Calvin, this was a doctrine of comfort. The Creator continues to rule over creation in all circumstances.

Book Two: The Knowledge of God the Redeemer in Christ

To redeem means to buy back; more specifically, it can mean to free or liberate by paying a ransom price. In Calvin's theology, just as in most traditional Christian teaching, Christ is the Redeemer, the one who pays the price for Christians that they may be liberated from sin and death.

Since Calvin wanted to explain God the Redeemer in Christ, he first had to spell out why it is that humans need redemption. Again following the interpretation of numerous Christians before him, Calvin read the story about Adam and Eve (found in Genesis, the first book of the Bible) as a literal fall from grace. They turned from God and brought sin into the world. From that point forward, sin became part of human nature. Though, of course, there might be individual acts of sin (lying, murder, etc.), sinful human nature was the basis of those acts; according to Calvin, the human being, after the Fall, is an essentially flawed creature.

As a result, both the understanding and will of humankind is warped. What should shine forth from nature—God's goodness and power—is neither seen nor understood, and the will to act in accord with God's goodness is twisted in the human soul. As a result, humanity can do nothing to please God or to properly glorify God. This means that all true knowledge of God is lost.

It is only through Christ the mediator, and through faith in him, that proper knowledge of God and God's goodness can be restored. Only through God the Redeemer in Christ can God the Creator be truly known. Thus, faith in God can only come through faith in Christ, for, according to Calvin, without Christ, God is unknowable.

For Calvin, the whole of Scripture points to Jesus Christ. The prophets of the Old Testament (how Christians refer to the Jewish Bible) foretold Christ; events within the sacred history of Israel foreshadowed Jesus; and the Law, the moral commands of the Old Testament, also showed forth the promise of salvation in Christ. Although Calvin thought the Law functioned in a number of ways to hold back the wicked, to convict of sin, to set forth punishment, its positive function was to hold forth the promise of a savior. Moreover, while the Law's power to condemn is nullified for those redeemed by Christ, it continues to be useful to Christians as a guide to grateful behavior. Hence, Calvin expounded at length on how the Ten Commandments— especially when one finds broad principles at work behind the specific commands—serve as helpful aids in living a holy life after redemption by Christ.

Although Calvin considered the whole Bible to bear witness to Christ, he taught that the fullest, clearest revelation of Christ came in the New Testament, in the gospel message. Whereas there are points of continuity between the Old Testament and the New—that Christ is the subject of both, that grace is revealed in both, that faith is the main point of both—Calvin thought that there were also some differences. Most of these have to do with the fact that the New Testament, according to Calvin, is a fuller, clearer revelation of Christ. It is as if the Old Testament were a pencil sketching and the gospel were a full-color picture.

Finally, Calvin used the rest of Book Two to write specifically about Christ and how to understand him. Christ is the mediator between God and humanity, sharing both a fully divine nature and a fully human nature. This is especially important for Calvin in that Christ is meant to bridge a gap between God, who by nature is above and beyond his creation, and humanity, who, even if there had never been a Fall, could not have reached God in his transcendence. As Calvin explained it, Jesus Christ is really and truly "Immanuel," a word that means "God with us." This, as Calvin understood it, is accomplished "in such a way that his divinity and our human nature might by mutual connection grow together. Otherwise the nearness would not have been near enough . . . to hope that God might dwell with us."[41]

This is the reason that Christ took on true human flesh. Without so doing, he could not have been the mediator between God and humanity, could not have been the Redeemer, and that, according to Calvin, was the whole purpose of Christ's incarnation: redemption. Thus, of necessity, Christ must be seen as fully human as well as fully divine: human that the distance between God and humanity could be bridged; divine that the power of God's righteousness could be bestowed on believers through Christ.

Calvin believed that Christ fulfilled his function as redeemer under a threefold office: prophet, priest, and king. As a prophet, Christ witnesses God's grace. As a priest, he intercedes on behalf of believers, making atonement for sin; as king, he rules a spiritual kingdom of the redeemed, forever caring for their needs.

Calvin was adamant that Christ's obedience unto death on a cross functioned to redeem. Christ's death served as the payment for sin; his descent into hell (something found in the statements of belief that date from the early church, for example, in the

Apostle's Creed and the Nicene Creed) represented the spiritual torment Christ was willing to endure to save his people. Through obedience and death, Christ merited God's grace and salvation for Christians. Why? Calvin answered simply: "God's grace . . . has ordained this manner of salvation for us."[42] Further speculation, Calvin thought, was simply an exhibition of ingratitude toward God.

Book Three: The Way in Which
We Receive the Grace of Christ

In Book Three, Calvin wrote at length about how grace is received, what benefits flow from it, and what effects follow.

Calvin insisted that the Holy Spirit works to seal the work of Christ on the heart of the Christian. It is "the secret energy of the Spirit, by which we come to enjoy Christ and all his benefits."[43]

The primary work of the Holy Spirt is the creation of faith. As with other Reformers of the sixteenth century, Calvin taught that Christians were saved by "faith alone." What, then, is this faith that the Spirit imprints upon the Christian?

"We hold faith to be a knowledge of God's will toward us, perceived from his Word."[44] The complicated way Calvin understood the concept of "God's Word" has been shown, but to pull all of the meanings together: The living Word (Christ) testified to in the written Word (Scripture), pronounced in the preached Word (the sermon), and exhibited through the visible Word (the Eucharist) all point to a loving God who promises grace. Thus, faith is the "firm and certain knowledge of God's benevolence [good will] toward us, founded upon the truth of the freely given promise in Christ, both revealed to our minds and sealed upon our hearts through the Holy Spirit."[45] Such faith, made possible through Christ, indeed, made real by a joining to Christ through the Holy Spirit, receives the grace of God's redemption.

Calvin believed that such faith, worked by the Holy Spirit, evoked repentance, a turning away from sin and toward God. Thus, once accepted by God through grace received in faith, the process of change starts, one that Calvin calls regeneration. The

Christian lives a life more in accord with God's will as a result of redemption because, as a child of God filled with thanksgiving, the Christian desires to live life in imitation of Christ. Having been justified by Christ, the Christian begins a life of sanctification, of holy living. So, for Calvin, the process of redemption was not simply a matter of "belief," at least not in just an intellectual way. As he declared, the gospel "is a doctrine not of the tongue but of life. It is not apprehended by the understanding and memory alone . . . but it is received only when it possesses the whole soul, and finds a seat and resting place in the inmost affection of the heart."[46]

Calvin proceeded to speak about Christian freedom; with rebirth, the Christian is free from the law because it is now written on the Christian's heart. The law can no longer condemn or produce guilt—it is now a guide by which the Christian's heart learns its true desires to serve God and fellow human beings.

Within the context of faith, Calvin teaches about prayer, relying heavily upon the Lord's Prayer ("Our Father, who art in heaven . . .") as a model. Prayer is a communion with God, a sign of trust, an instrument of perseverance.

Much has been made of Calvin's doctrine of predestination, which appears near the end of Book Three. It is a thorny and complicated topic, with a long history in Christian thought. The word means that God chooses who will be redeemed. Almost all of the early Protestants held to some form of this teaching. Some of the most respected teachers of the Catholic tradition— St. Augustine and St. Thomas Aquinas, for example—also defended the doctrine. Calvin himself thought it properly understood from within the context of faith; that's why it is in Book Three. Calvin thought many passages in the Bible supported the notion of predestination, and he thought the concept also explained some things in the world around him (such as, if everyone thought the gospel a good thing, as most said, why did everyone not live in a way consistent with the gospel?). If God's grace, as Calvin thought, was truly absolutely free, then there could be no question of earning it, not even by taking so little a step as accepting grace as a gift by one's own will power. Calvin believed even the acceptance of salvation involved the work of the Holy Spirit working within the Christian, rather than the Christian choosing for him or herself.

Though many have a difficult time accepting or understanding predestination—whether it is Calvin's version or some other—it should be said that Calvin himself always found it a doctrine of comfort, for he believed that God had chosen him, and having chosen him, God would always abide with him no matter what. He likewise thought it would be a comfort to all true Christians, for it placed their salvation not in their own weak hands but in God's almighty hand.

Book Four: The External Means or Aids

Though this section takes up a large portion of the *Institutes*, the concerns of the book can be easily cataloged.

Within this part, Calvin dealt with what helps a Christian in his or her life of faith. How has God provided, once union with Christ has taken place, for the Christian to find support in that new life?

First of all, God has ordained that there should be a gathering of Christians known as the church. Calvin understood the church to be, in a sense, the schoolhouse of the Christian, where he or she learned the fundamentals of the faith and then progressed to greater and greater maturity, understanding, and love.

Within the church, God provides for the ministry of the Word. That is, God calls forth preachers whom God uses to proclaim the good news of the gospel.

Intermixed with the many constructive things Calvin has to say about the church and its ministry is the condemnation of the practices of the Catholic Church. Though Calvin never denies that there are Christians in the Catholic Church, he does insist that the structure, practices, and ministry of the Catholic Church had attached to them hundreds of years of accumulated human-made traditions. The whole purpose of reform, in Calvin's mind, was to strip those human traditions away so that only the gospel dictated what true worship, ministry, and church would be like.

For Calvin, the true church existed wherever the Word of God was preached and the sacraments (baptism and the Lord's Supper) rightly administered. He also believed the church needed to discipline its members, but he did not make that a mark of the true church.

The sacraments, according to Calvin, are those rituals instituted by Christ that attest to the promises Christ has made having to do with salvation, and they do so in such as way as to impress upon the believer's heart the truth of those promises. In baptism, there is the promise that sin can be washed away and that one can be raised to new life with Christ. The water serves as a symbol of cleansing.

The Eucharist, the memorial meal that reenacts Jesus' Last Supper with his disciples, promises forgiveness of sin. The breaking of the bread and the pouring of wine symbolize the breaking of Christ's body on the cross and the outpouring of his blood—redemptive acts, according to Calvin. Furthermore, by eating the bread and drinking the wine, Christians are assured that Christ has joined himself to them in the most intimate way, so that they partake of Christ himself, to the point that there is a communion between the two wherein Christ shares his righteousness with the believers.

After Calvin explained how he understood the sacraments, he attacked the Catholic Church's teaching on the sacraments, and he argued that the number of sacraments is only two, not seven, as the Catholic Church taught.

Calvin ended the *Institutes* with a very interesting chapter on civil government. Just as the work began addressing a king, so it ends speaking about government. Calvin, like many of his time, was afraid of anarchy—the absence of rulers and government. Nor did he trust democracy, because of his dim view of human nature. He believed rulers held their positions directly because God has so ordained. He thought citizens should obey their rulers. Despite this outlook, however, Calvin would not cede absolute authority to civil government.

Once called "The Constructive Revolutionary,"[47] Calvin did allow that, whereas citizens could not rise up against their government, there were those who could lawfully depose a tyrant—those who served beneath the ruler. Those who lawfully held positions of authority under a ruler could be used by God to overthrow a government. In other words, Calvin allowed for a transfer of power within government, even one by force, if undertaken by the right people.

Still, no government or ruler had absolute control. In the last section of the book, Calvin warned that God, rather than human rulers, must be obeyed. As he declared in the very last line of the *Institutes,* "We have been redeemed by Christ at so great a price . . . so . . . we should not enslave ourselves to the wicked desires of men much less be subject to their impiety."[48] On that note, then, Calvin closed his great work on the sum of all piety.

9

Calvin's Legacy

*All modern Western history would have been unrecognizably
different without the perpetual play of Calvin's influence.*

—John T. McNeill,
The History and Character of Calvinism

H istorical assessments of John Calvin have been notoriously divided. In his own time, there were those, such as John Knox, the great Scottish reformer, who thought that studying with Calvin in Geneva was like the most perfect school of Christ's apostles. On the other hand, others, such as Jerome Bolsec, the man we read about in a previous chapter who was exiled from Geneva because of a theological disagreement with Calvin, wrote in his very negative biography of Calvin that he was the tyrant of Geneva. These are two very different views.

Later in time, the world's assessment of Calvin continued to be as severely divided. The Swiss thinker Karl Barth, considered by many to be the greatest Protestant theologian of the twentieth century and who deeply infuenced a church movement that, at great risk, stood up to and confronted Hitler and Nazism, said that he could profitably spend his entire life wrapped up in the study of Calvin. On the other hand, another Swiss thinker, Jacob Burckhardt, stated that nothing worse could have happened to Reformation Europe than that John Calvin became one of Protestantism's leaders after the death of Martin Luther.

Today, Calvin continues to have devoted followers and tenacious detractors. At least in the United States, this has partly to do with a culture war of the nineteenth century, when certain writers and thinkers sought to overthrow what they saw as the remnants of the Calvinist culture of New England (New England's Calvinism came primarily through the Puritans, who brought to the United States a Reformed Protestantism). These writers, especially in novels, were able to reinforce and continue stereotypes of Calvinists as unhappy, unbending, grim apostles of a severe religion. At the same time, however, it has been noted by more than one person that the longest intellectual tradition in the United States is rooted in a type of Calvinism.

Stereotypes of Calvin continue, though scholars of John Calvin's life have debunked many of the myths that surround the notion of the "tyrant of Geneva": The execution of Servetus, when put in historical context, does not mark Calvin as especially vicious, and there has been a recovery of some aspects of life in the city of Geneva that point to the Consistory's attempt to make Geneva a civil environment. Though scholars have painted a much more nuanced portrait of Calvin than that presented in many history textbooks, which simply perpetuate the old stereotypes, Calvin's name still evokes strong reaction, either for him or against him.

Perhaps, in the end, there is simply a personality that emerges from Calvin's work: Some are drawn to it, some are not. He was a man of strong opinions, and he and his followers took action on what they understood to be the truth. This happens both within Christianity and within other religions. Perhaps one could afford to Calvin the same attitude he once afforded to Luther (Luther drew criticism from many for his lifestyle, way of speaking, and temper when writing against opponents): "Ah Luther! How few imitators of your excellence have you left," Calvin declared, "how many apes of your holy boasting." [49] Calvin looked to hold up the good in Luther while discouraging people from following his excesses.

Regardless of how one ends up assessing Calvin the person, there is, apart from that, the question of Calvin the historical force: He had an influence, and it was sweeping and far-reaching. This influence ranges from the establishment of churches to the development of religious thought to political and social consequences. Indeed, as has been said, "All modern Western history would have been unrecognizably different without the perpetual play of Calvin's influence." [50]

Without a doubt, Calvinism became an international movement. Whereas Lutheranism was by and large contained in the Holy Roman Empire (much later to become Germany) and the Scandinavian countries, Calvinism spread throughout Europe. In some places, it became the predominant religion; in others, it lived as a minority religion. Regardless of whether a majority or minority, however, Calvinists were often quite active in society and a force with which to be reckoned. They often exhibited the same tough-mindedness as their religious forebear.

One could find Calvinist congregations in the Holy Roman Empire, France, and the Swiss city-states; they were firmly entrenched in the low countries, especially Holland. In Eastern Europe, one could (and can still) find Calvinist communities, although in most areas they were brutally suppressed. Across the channel, Calvinists became the majority religion in Scotland, and they became a powerful minority in England (actually over-throwing the king in the mid-seventeenth century and setting up their own government under Oliver Cromwell). Eventually, the Calvinist tradition made its way to the United States in the guise of Puritanism, but others came who were not Puritan. Dutch Calvinists came and settled in New York and New Jersey; another such group migrated to Michigan around the Grand Rapids area. In another time, the Dutch took their Calvinism with them to South Africa.

Calvinism as an expression of Reformed Protestantism con-tinues to spread to this day. One of the hotbeds of such growth is in South Korea. There, Korean Presbyterians (Presbyterians are one of the Christian denominations that look to Calvin as a foundational influence) share the gospel using a Calvinist framework. Indeed, some of the works that are a must-read for Calvin scholars come out of Korean Calvinism.

Some have argued, however, that Calvinism's influence goes beyond the simple establishment of congregations. There are those who have seen in Calvinism a world-affirming view that values work in the world, and these values contributed to the development and expansion of capitalism. Others have seen a commitment to freedom of conscience, which has helped strong antiauthoritarian views emerge. Still others see Calvinism's fingerprints all over such things as the U.S. Constitution, the political order of the United States, the development of education systems in the United States, and the creation of civil religion in the United States—those shared core values that are invoked by presidents in religious terms when they speak to the nation, especially in times of crisis. Although the notion of the United States as a "city set upon a hill" was first articulated by the Puritan John Winthrop before there was a United States, the phrase has become a stock line in the speeches of contemporary U.S. presidents.

Remarking on such indicators of cultural influence, Alister McGrath has written, "The full history of the impact of Calvinism upon Western culture has yet to be written." He goes on to say, however, that enough is known of the ways Calvinism has influenced that culture that one can say, "to study Calvin is not merely to study the past—it is also to gain a deeper understanding of the present. . . . Although Calvin lies buried in an unmarked grave somewhere in Geneva, his ideas and influence live on in the outlooks of the culture he helped to create."[51]

John Calvin saw himself as a timid scholar who had been called by God to help reform church life in the city of Geneva. Yet, his work as a spiritual leader and thinker catapulted him into the spotlight of Western history, where many still study him and his influence in order to understand Western religion, society, and culture.

APPENDIX

The First Chapter of Book One in Calvin's
Institutes of the Christian Religion

BOOK ONE

The Knowledge of God the Creator

Chapter 1

THE KNOWLEDGE OF GOD AND THAT OF OURSELVES ARE CONNECTED. HOW THEY ARE INTERRELATED

1. *Without knowledge of self there is no knowledge of God*

Nearly all the wisdom we possess, that is to say, true and sound wisdom, consists of two parts: the knowledge of God and of ourselves. But, while joined by many bonds, which one precedes and brings forth the other is not easy to discern. In the first place, no one can look upon himself without immediately turning his thoughts to the contemplation of God, in whom he "lives and moves" [Acts 17:28]. For, quite clearly, the mighty gifts with which we are endowed are hardly from ourselves; indeed, our very being is nothing but subsistence in the one God. Then, by these benefits shed like dew from heaven upon us, we are led as by rivulets to the spring itself. Indeed, our very poverty better discloses the infinitude of benefits reposing in God. The miserable ruin, into which the rebellion of the first man cast us, especially compels us to look upward. Thus, not only will we, in fasting and hungering, seek thence what we lack; but, in being aroused by fear we shall learn humility. For, as a veritable world of miseries is to be found in mankind, and we are thereby despoiled of divine raiment, our shameful nakedness exposes a teeming horde of infamies. Each of us must, then, be so stung by the consciousness of his own unhappiness as to attain at least some knowledge of God. Thus, from the feeling of our own ignorance, vanity, poverty, infirmity, and, what is more, depravity and corruption, we recognize that the true light of wisdom, sound virtue, full abundance of every good, and purity of righteousness rest in the Lord alone. To this extent we are prompted by our own ills to contemplate the good things of God; and we cannot seriously aspire to him before we begin to become displeased with ourselves. For what man in all the world would not gladly remain as he is—what man does not remain as he is —so long as he does not know himself, that is, while content with his own gifts, and either ignorant or unmindful of his own misery? Accordingly, the knowledge of ourselves not only arouses us to seek God, but also, as it were, leads us by the hand to find him.

APPENDIX

The First Chapter of Book Four in Calvin's
Institutes of the Christian Religion

BOOK FOUR

The External Means or Aims by Which God
Invites Us Into the Society of Christ
and Holds Us Therein

Chapter 1

THE TRUE CHURCH WITH WHICH AS MOTHER OF ALL THE GODLY WE MUST KEEP UNITY

(The Holy Catholic Church, our mother, 1–4)

1. *The necessity of the church*

As explained in the previous book, it is by the faith in the gospel that Christ becomes ours and we are made partakers of the salvation and eternal blessedness brought by him. Since, however, in our ignorance and sloth (to which I add fickleness of disposition) we need outward helps to beget and increase faith within us, and advance it to its goal, God has also added these aids that he may provide for our weakness. And in order that the preaching of the gospel might flourish, he deposited this treasure in the church. He instituted "pastors and teachers" [Eph. 4:11] through whose lips he might teach his own; he furnished them with authority; finally, he omitted nothing that might make for holy agreement of faith and for right order. First of all, he instituted sacraments, which we who have experienced them feel to be highly useful aids to foster and strengthen faith. Shut up as we are in the prison house of our flesh, we have not yet attained angelic rank. God, therefore, in his wonderful providence accommodating himself to our capacity, has prescribed a way for us, though still far off, to draw near to him.

Accordingly, our plan of instruction now requires us to discuss the church, its government, orders, and power; then the sacraments; and lastly, the civil order. At the same time we are to call back godly readers from those corruptions by which Satan, in the papacy, has polluted everything God had appointed for our salvation.

I shall start, then, with the church, into whose bosom God is pleased to gather his sons, not only that they may be nourished by her help and ministry as long as they are infants and children, but also that they may be guided by the motherly care until they mature and at last reach the goal of faith. "For what God has joined together, it is not lawful to put asunder" [Mark 10:9 p.], so that, for those to whom he is Father the church may also be Mother. And this was so not only under the law but also after Christ's coming, as Paul testifies when he teaches that we are the children of the new and heavenly Jerusalem [Gal. 4:26].

APPENDIX

From Calvin's *New Testament Commentaries*

CHAPTER ELEVEN

Now faith is the assurance of things hoped for,
the proving of things not seen.

1. *Now faith is*

Whoever made this the beginning of the eleventh chapter broke up the sequence wrongly. The purpose of the apostle is to support what he has said, that there is need for patience. He has quoted the testimony of Habakkuk who says that the just shall live by his faith. He now shows what remained that faith can no more be separated from patience than from itself. The sequence of his thought is this: we shall never arrive at the goal of salvation unless we are furnished with patience. The prophet declares that the just shall live by faith, but faith calls us to far off things which we have not yet attained; and therefore it necessarily includes patience in itself. The minor proposition in the syllogism is: *faith is the substance, etc.* It is clear from this that those who think that an exact definition of faith is being given here are greatly mistaken. The apostle is not discussing the nature of faith as a whole but he selects that part which fits his purpose, namely that it is always joined to patience.

Let us now consider the words. He calls it the substance of things hoped for. We know that what is hoped for is not what is in our hand but what is so far hidden from us or at least the enjoyment of which is put off to another time. The apostle is saying the same thing as Paul in Rom. 8.24, where after he has said that what is hoped for is not seen, he draws the conclusion that it is waited for in patience. Thus our apostle teaches us that we do not have faith in God from things present but from the expectation of things still to come. The appearance of this contradiction is not without its charm. He says that faith is the substance, that is, the prop or the foundation on which we place our feet; but of what? Of things absent which are so far from being under our feet that they far exceed the power of our understanding to capture.

The same idea runs through the second clause where he calls faith the evidence, that is the demonstration of things not seen. A demonstration makes things appear, and commonly refers only to what is subject to our senses. These two things apparently contradict each other, but yet they agree perfectly when we are concerned with faith. The Spirit of God shows us hidden things, the knowledge of which cannot reach our senses. Eternal life is promised to us, but it is promised to the dead; we are told of the resurrection of the blessed, but meantime we are involved in corruption, we are declared to be just, and sin dwells within us; we hear that we are blessed, but meantime we are overwhelmed by untold miseries; we are promised an abundance of all good things, but we are often hungry and thirsty; God proclaims that He will come to us immediately, but seems to be deaf to our cries. What would happen to us if we did not rely on our hope, and if our minds did not emerge above the world out of the midst of darkness through the shining Word of God and by His Spirit? Faith is therefore rightly called the substance of things which are still the objects of hope and the evidence of things not seen. Augustine sometimes interchanges evidence and conviction, and I do not disagree, for that faithfully expresses the mind of the apostle. I prefer the noun 'demonstration' or 'evidence', because it is less forced.

From Calvin's *Short Treatise on the Holy Supper of Our Lord Jesus Christ*

5. JESUS CHRIST THE ONLY SPIRITUAL NOURISHMENT OF OUR SOULS

We have already seen that Jesus Christ is the only food by which our souls are nourished; but as it is distributed to us by the word of the Lord, which he has appointed an instrument for that purpose, that word is also called bread and water. Now what is said of the word applies as well to the sacrament of the Supper, by means of which the Lord leads us to communion with Jesus Christ. For seeing we are so weak that we cannot receive him with true heartfelt trust, when he is presented to us by simple doctrine and preaching, the Father of mercy, disdaining not to condescend in this matter of our infirmity, has been pleased to add to his word a visible sign, by which he might represent the substance of his promises, to confirm and fortify us by delivering us from all doubt and uncertainty. Since, then, there is something so mysterious and incomprehensible in saying that we have communion with the body and the blood of Jesus Christ, and we on our part are so rude and gross that we cannot understand the least things of God, it was of importance that we should be given to understand it as far as our capacity could admit.

6. THE CAUSE WHY OUR LORD INSTITUTED THE SUPPER

Our Lord, therefore, instituted the Supper, first, in order to sign and seal in our consciences the promises contained in his gospel concerning our being made partakers of his body and blood, and to give us certainty and assurance that therein lies our true spiritual nourishment, and that having such an earnest, we may entertain a right reliance of salvation. Secondly, in order to exercise us in recognizing his great goodness toward us, and thus lead us to laud and magnify him more fully. Thirdly, in order to exhort us to all holiness and innocence, inasmuch as we are members of Jesus Christ; and specially to exhort us to union and brotherly charity, as we are expressly commanded. When we shall have well considered these three reasons, to which the Lord had respect in ordaining his Supper, we shall be able to understand, both what benefit accrues to us from it, and what is our duty in order to use it properly.

APPENDIX

THE DEITY OF JESUS CHRIST

> *In the beginning was the Word, and the Word was with*
> *God, and the Word was God. He was in the beginning*
> *with God. All things were made by him, and without*
> *him nothing was made that was made. In him was life,*
> *and the life was the light of men. The light shines in*
> *darkness, and the darkness comprehended it not.*

THE WORD "Gospel" declares how God loved us when He sent our Lord Jesus Christ into the world. We must note this well. For it is important to know how Holy Scripture uses words. Surely we need not stop simply at words, but we cannot understand the teaching of God unless we know what procedure, style and language He uses. We have to note this word, all the more since it is such a common practice to refer to Holy Scripture as the Law and the Gospel. Those who speak thus intend that all the promises contained in the Old Testament should be referred to the word "Gospel." Surely their intention is good, but Holy Scripture does not speak thus of itself. We should be careful and out of reverence for the Spirit of God retain the manner of speaking which He uses to instruct us.

The word "Gospel" indicates that God in sending our Lord Jesus Christ His Son declares Himself Father to all the world. St. Paul writes to the Ephesians that Jesus Christ came to evangelize those who were near and those who were far from God. Those near were the Jews, who were already allied with God. Those far were the pagans who were aloof from His Church. When we have looked at it in the light of all Scripture we shall find that this word "Gospel" has no other meaning.

That is why this word is the title of the four written histories of how our Lord Jesus Christ came into the world, He went about, He died, He rose again, He ascended into heaven. That, I

say, comes under the title "Gospel." And why all that? Because
the substance of the Gospel is comprehended in the Person of
the Son of God, as I have already said. The Ancient Fathers
surely had the promises of salvation. They were well assured that
God would be their Father. But they did not have the Guarantee
for the love of God and for their adoption. For when Jesus
Christ came into the world, God signed and sealed His fatherly
love. We have received full testimony of life, the substance of
which (as I have already said) we have in Jesus Christ. That is
why St. Paul says that all the promises of God are in Him, Yea
and Amen. For God then ratified all that He had previously said
and had promised to men.

So not without cause those four histories have been named
"Gospel," where it is declared to us how the Son of God was sent,
He took human flesh, and He went about with men in this life.
All that is comprehended under the name "Gospel," because it
declares to us how God perfected and accomplished everything
which was required for the salvation of men, and it was all done
in the Person of His Son.

St. Paul can well speak of his gospel, but how so? It is not that
he has written a Gospel history, but that his teaching conformed
to all that is herein contained. Thus, following what I have
already said, when the Gospel is proclaimed to us, it is a manifestation of Jesus Christ, so that in Him we may know that all
things are perfected and that we have the truth of that which had
been promised from all time. But for all that the Epistles of
St. Paul are not named "Gospel." And why not? Because there we
have not a continuous history which shows us how God sent His
Son, how He willed that assuming our nature he might have true
brotherhood with us, how He died, was raised, and ascended
into heaven. These things, I say, are not deduced from a single,
continuous thread in Saint Paul. It is very certain that the
teaching which is contained in his Epistles is conformed to
the teaching of the Gospel. But for all that the word is especially ascribed to these four histories, for the reason that I have
already alleged.

Now when we say that the substance of the Gospel is comprehended in the Person of the Son of God, that is not only to say that Jesus Christ has come into the world, but that we may know also His office, the charge committed to Him by God His Father, and His power.

Let us note the difference between the Gospel according to St. John and the other three. The four Gospel-writers are entirely agreed in that they declare how the Son of God appeared in the world, that He has been made true man, like us in all things except sin. Next they describe how He died, He rose again, and He ascended into heaven. Briefly, all that was committed to Him to draw us to God His Father is there declared.

But there are two things which are peculiar to Saint John. One is that he pays more attention to the teaching of Jesus Christ than do the others. Likewise, he declares to us with greater liveliness His virtue and His power. Surely the others relate well the teaching of Jesus Christ, but more briefly. Little summaries in the others appear as long declarations in Saint John. For example, in chapter 6 we see what is said of the miracle He did in the desert, when He fed such a multitude. From that Saint John leads up to the proposition that Jesus Christ is the Bread of Life Eternal. We see this teaching of Jesus Christ which is expounded at length by Saint John, and with a greater deduction that is made by the other Gospel-writers, and which was even omitted by them. So it is throughout. For after he has mentioned certain miracles and stories he always comes back to the teaching and finds occasion to put in material treating on the virtue of our Lord Jesus Christ. From chapter 12 to the narrative of the Passion he treats only of that teaching.

We see now the difference between the Gospel according to Saint John and the other three. To say it better, the Gospel according to Saint John is to us, as it were, the key by which we enter into an understanding of the others. For if we read Saint Matthew, Saint Mark, and Saint Luke we shall not know so well why Jesus Christ was sent into the world as when we shall have read Saint John. Having read Saint John, we shall know then how what our Lord Jesus Christ has done benefits us, that He took human flesh, that He died and rose again. We shall learn, I say, the purpose and the substance of all those things in reading this Gospel. That is why he does not linger over the story, as we shall see by the order which he follows. Surely these things ought to be considered more at length, but since there is much substance to the text we have to expound, I mention things as briefly as I can.

1509   John Calvin is born in Noyon, France, on July 10.

1516   Concordat of Bologna is signed.

1517   Martin Luther's "Ninety-Five Theses" are posted.

1520   Luther publishes his Reformation Treatises.

1521   Luther is excommunicated; Protestant Christianity begins.

1523   Calvin goes to college in Paris at the College of Montaigu.

1528–1531   Calvin attends law school at Orléans, then Bourges, then returns to Orléans.

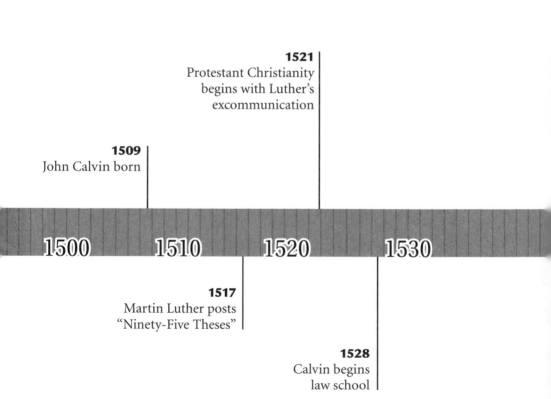

1521
Protestant Christianity
begins with Luther's
excommunication

1509
John Calvin born

1500   1510   1520   1530

1517
Martin Luther posts
"Ninety-Five Theses"

1528
Calvin begins
law school

1532 In April, Calvin self-publishes his commentary on Seneca's *On Clemency*.

1533 On November 1, Nicholas Cop gives his inaugural address, which favors reform at the University of Paris (many think Calvin wrote it); those known to be connected with the ideas of reform are forced to flee Paris.

1534 In May, Calvin travels to his hometown, Noyon, and resigns his benefice; in October, the Affair of the Placards takes place; there is a swift reaction against Protestants in France.

1535
Calvin completes the first edition of *Institutes*, written in Latin

1564
Calvin dies on May 27

1537
Calvin appointed Reader of Holy Scripture and later a pastor in Geneva

1535   1545   1555   1565

1539
Expanded, reorganized edition of *Institutes* is published

1559
The fifth edition of Latin version of *Institutes* is published

1545
Another major revised edition of *Institutes* is published

1550
The fourth edition of Latin version of *Institutes* is published

1535 In January, Calvin is in Basel, where he completes the first edition of his *Institutes of the Christian Religion*; the dedication page is dated September 10, 1535.

1536 In March, the first edition of the *Institutes* is published; during the summer, Calvin is back in France for a few months; in August, Calvin finds himself in Geneva, where Farel persuades him to stay and help with reform.

1537 In January, Calvin is appointed Reader in Holy Scripture by the city council; he is later appointed pastor as well; Calvin and Farel present the city council with articles for the organization of the church.

1538 In April, after Easter, Calvin and Farel are forced to leave Geneva because of a conflict with the city council; in September, Calvin moves from Basel to Strasbourg to minister to French refugees, serving at the request of Martin Bucer.

1539 A new edition of the *Institutes* is published; the *Reply to Sadolet* is produced.

1540 Calvin publishes his first biblical commentary, on Romans (many more commentaries on various books would follow through the coming years); during the summer, Calvin marries Idelette de Bure.

1541 A French translation of the *Institutes* is published; the *Short Treatise on the Holy Supper of Our Lord Jesus Christ* is published; in September, Calvin returns to Geneva; a draft of ecclesiastical ordinances is presented to the city council.

1545 Another major revision of the *Institutes* is published.

1549 Calvin's wife, Idelette de Bure, dies; the Agreement of Zurich is signed.

1550 The fourth revision of the Latin *Institutes* is published.

1553 Servetus is executed.

1555 A pro-Calvin city council is elected.

1559 The final Latin edition of the *Institutes* is published; the Genevan Academy is opened; Theodore Beza comes to Geneva; Calvin finally becomes a citizen of Geneva.

1560 The final French edition of the *Institutes* is published.

1564 May 27 Calvin dies; Beza is named as his successor.

NOTES

CHAPTER 1:
Pulled into the Spotlight

1. John Calvin, "Preface" to the *Commentary on the Book of Psalms*, in *Selected Writings of John Calvin*, ed. John Dillenberger. Missoula, Mont.: Scholars Press, 1975, p. 28.

2. Cited in Thomas J. Davis, *The Clearest Promises of God: The Development of Calvin's Eucharistic Teaching*. New York: AMS Press, 1995, p. 8, note 1. There is still some defense of this sentiment: See Alister E. McGrath, *A Life of John Calvin: A Study in the Shaping of Western Culture*. Oxford, England: Basil Blackwell, 1990, pp. 145–147.

3. William J. Bouwsma, "A World Out of Joint." Chap. 3 in *John Calvin: A Sixteenth Century Portrait*. Oxford, England: Oxford University Press, 1988.

4. This was a book called *Julius Excluded*, probably written by a famous Christian humanist named Erasmus. The first dated edition was published in 1518, though undated editions appeared before that year. Many date the writing somewhere around 1513.

CHAPTER 2:
Growing Up as the World Changes: 1509–1527

5. Most scholars date Calvin's entry into college as 1523. See, for example, Alexandre Ganoczy, *The Young Calvin*, trans. David Foxgrover and Wade Provo. Philadelphia, Penn.: Westminster Press, 1987, p. 57. A few people, however, place Calvin in Paris as early as 1520 or 1521, when he would have been 11 or 12 years old. See T.H.L. Parker, *John Calvin*. Tring, England, and Batavia, Ill.: Lion Publishing, 1987, p. 188.

CHAPTER 3:
From Lawyer to Protestant Reformer: 1528–1535

6. McGrath, p. 59.

7. John Calvin, *Institutes of the Christian Religion, 1536 Edition*, rev. ed., trans. Ford Lewis Battles. Grand Rapids, Mich.: Wm. B. Eerdmans Publishing, 1986, p. 1.

8. Ibid.

9. Ibid., p. 17.

10. Ibid., p. 43.

CHAPTER 4:
Learning to Be a Leader: 1536–1541

11. William G. Naphy, *Calvin and the Consolidation of the Genevan Reformation*. Louisville, Ky.: Westminster John Knox Press, 2003, p. 20.

12. McGrath, p. 102.

13. "Romans 1:17," in *The New Oxford Annotated Bible with the Apocrypha, Revised Standard Version*, ed. Herbert G. May and Bruce M. Metzger. New York: Oxford University Press, 1977.

14. Parker, p. 92.

CHAPTER 5:
Calvin's Return to Geneva and the Establishment of a Reformed Church: 1541–1549

15. John Calvin, *Reply to Letter by Cardinal Sadolet to the Senate and Peole of Geneva*, in Calvin, *Selected Writings*, p. 115.

16. Ibid., p. 83.

17. John Calvin, *Selected Works of John Calvin*, 7 vols., ed. Jules Bonnet, trans. David Constable. Grand Rapids, Mich.: Baker Book House, 1983, 4:212.

18. Ibid., 4:187.

19. This analysis is based on the work of Charles M. Cooke, M.D., "Calvin's Illnesses and Their Relation to Christian Vocation," in *Calvin Studies IV*, ed. John Leith and W. Stacy Johnson. Davidson, N.C.: Davidson College, 1988, pp. 41–52. Though these medical problems began to appear in the late 1540s, by the mid-1550s, acute pain and extreme difficulty in breathing characterized Calvin's existence.

20. Bouwsma argues from solid evidence that Calvin and his wife had at least three children, and perhaps four. See Bouwsma, p. 23.

CHAPTER 6:
Calvin's Geneva: 1550–1564

21. Parker, p. 137.

22. Naphy, p. 144.

23. Ibid., p. 150.

24. McGrath, p. 116.

25. John Calvin, "Calvin's Will and Address to the Magistrates and Ministers," in Calvin, Selected Writings, p. 36.

26. Ibid., pp. 35–36.

CHAPTER 7:
Calvin and the Word of God

27. John Calvin, The Mystery of Godliness and Other Selected Sermons. Grand Rapids, Mich.: Wm. B. Eerdmans, 1950, p. 17.

28. John Calvin, The Gospel According to John, Part One, 1–10, trans. T.H.L. Parker. Edinburgh, Scotland: Oliver and Boyd, 1961; reprinted, Grand Rapids, Mich.: Wm. B. Eerdmans, 1975, p. 167.

29. Willem van't Spijker, "Calvin's Friendship with Martin Bucer," in Calvin Studies Society Papers, 1995–1997: Calvin and Spirituality; Calvin and His Contemporaries, ed. David Foxgrover. Grand Rapids, Mich.: CSS, 1998, p. 174.

30. John Calvin, The Epistles of Paul to the Romans and Thessalonians, trans. Ross McKenzie. Edinburgh, Scotland: Oliver and Boyd, 1963; reprint, Grand Rapids, Mich.: Wm. B. Eerdmans, 1973, p. 231.

31. Calvin, The Mystery of Godliness, p. 25.

32. Ibid., p. 48.

33. B. A. Gerrish, "John Calvin and the Reformed Doctrine of the Lord's Supper," McCormick Quarterly 22 (1969): p. 92.

34. John Calvin, The Epistles of Paul the Apostle to the Galatians, Ephesians, Philippians, and Colossians, translated by T.H.L. Parker. Edinburgh, Scotland: Oliver and Boyd, 1965; reprint, Grand Rapids, Mich.: Wm. B. Eerdmans, 1965, pp. 209–210.

35. Brian A. Gerrish, Grace and Gratitude: The Eucharistic Theology of John Calvin. Minneapolis, Minn.: Fortress Press, 1993, p. 20.

CHAPTER 8:
Calvin's Theology

36. François Wendel, Calvin: The Origins and Development of His Religious Thought, trans. Philip Mairet. London: Wm. Collins Sons, 1963, p. 111, quoting Imbart de la Tour.

37. John Calvin, Institutes of the Christian Religion, 2 vols., ed. John T. McNeill and trans. Ford Lewis Battles. Philadelphia, Penn.: Westminster Press, 1960. 1.1.3

38. Institutes 1.4.4.

39. Institutes 1.5.10.

40. Institutes 1.6.1.

41. Institutes 2.12.1.

42. Institutes 2.17.1.

43. Institutes 3.1.1.

44. Institutes 3.2.6.

45. Institutes 3.2.7.

46. Institutes 3.6.4.

47. W. Fred Graham, The Constructive Revolutionary: John Calvin and His Socio-Economic Impact, paperback ed. Atlanta, Ga.: John Knox Press, 1978.

48. Institutes 4.20.32.

CHAPTER 9:
Calvin's Legacy

49. Calvin, Selected Works, 2:325. Again, in assessing Luther, Calvin thought Luther's gifts should be appreciated, but then he went on to say "to extol his defects as if they were virtues is foolish." Ibid., 2:477.

50. John T. McNeill, The History and Character of Calvinism. New York: Oxford University Press, 1954, p. 234.

51. McGrath, p. 261.

GLOSSARY

Anti-trinitarian—One who does not believe in the concept of the Trinity, which holds that there is one God in three persons: the Father, the Son, and the Holy Spirit.

Apology—A work that serves to justify or defend a principle or idea.

Baptism—A sacrament in which water is used ritualistically to admit an individual into the Christian community and to signify the forgiveness of sins.

Canon Law—The laws governing a church.

Catechism—Instructions in the principles of Christian faith, often in a question and answer format.

Catholic Church—Typically refers to the Roman Catholic Church, with its base in the Vatican; the Catholic Church is one of the first Christian churches and the one from which the Protestants divided in the sixteenth century.

Christendom—The idea that the institutions of Christianity worked with the various machineries of state (kings, princes, dukes, war leaders, etc.) to rule society; the nation of Christian society.

Communion—Also *Lord's Supper* or *Eucharist*. Of the seven sacraments in the Catholic Church, Calvin recognized only two, including Communion (Baptism is the second); Communion involves consuming bread and wine in celebration of the Last Supper, during which Jesus distributed bread and wine as his "body and blood."

Conciliarism—The idea that the true head of the church is a duly constituted council of the church.

Doctrine—The core beliefs of a religion.

Excommunication—An exclusion of a particular member from a community; in the case of those excommunicated from the church, this typically involved being denied access to the sacraments, most notably Communion.

Gospel—The teachings or Word of Christ; also the first four books of the New Testament (Matthew, Mark, Luke, and John).

Great Schism—After the French forcibly moved the pope to the French-controlled Avignon, France, in the fourteenth century, other countries sought to regain control of the papacy and installed a new pope in Rome, leading to the splintering of the Catholic Church between the two popes.

Humanism—A movement that valued the intellectual heritage and languages of the classical world. Emphasis placed on the restoration of correct and elegant Latin (as well as Greek). For Christian humanists, it meant the recovery of biblical languages and the writings of early Christians.

Lord's Supper—see *Communion*.

New Testament—In the Christian Bible, the 27 books that tell about the life of Jesus Christ, his death and resurrection, and the meaning of Chistian life, faith, and community.

Old Testament—The sacred scripture of the Jewish people, written mostly in Hebrew, it was incorporated into the Christian Bible as the "old" testament, that is, the testament (covenant) God had enacted before the coming of Christ, whom Christians thought initiated a "new" covenant (testament).

Piety—Religious devotion and duty.

Pope—The religious head of the Roman Catholic Church.

Predestination—The belief that God chooses or "elects" who will receive his gift of salvation.

Protestant—Literally, "one who protests"; the umbrella term used to classify Christians who are not members of the Roman Catholic or Eastern Church. Originally, it was used by Catholics as a term of derision starting in the late 1520s.

Reformation—The movement to reform the Catholic Church in the sixteenth century that resulted in the abandonment of some practices (such as the selling of indulgences) and the establishment of Protestant churches.

Sacrament—A Christian rite believed to be ordained by Jesus Christ. Of the seven that the Catholic Church recognizes, Calvin only recognized two: Communion and Baptism.

BIBLIOGRAPHY

WRITINGS OF JOHN CALVIN IN ENGLISH TRANSLATION

Calvin, John. *The Epistles of Paul the Apostle to the Galatians, Ephesians, Philippians, and Colossians.* Translated by T.H.L. Parker. Edinburgh, Scotland: Oliver and Boyd, 1965. Reprint, Grand Rapids, Mich.: Wm. B. Eerdmans, 1965.

————. *The Epistles of Paul to the Romans and Thessalonians.* Translated by Ross McKenzie. Edinburgh, Scotland: Oliver and Boyd, 1963. Reprint, Grand Rapids, Mich.: Wm. B. Eerdmans, 1973.

————. *The Gospel According to John, Part One, 1–10.* Translated by T.H.L. Parker. Edinburgh, Scotland: Oliver and Boyd, 1961. Reprint, Grand Rapids, Mich.: Wm. B. Eerdmans, 1975.

————. *Institutes of the Christian Religion.* Edited by John T. McNeill. Translated by Ford Lewis Battles. 2 vols. Philadelphia, Penn.: Westminster Press, 1960. This is the standard English translation of the 1559 *Institutes*, originally written in Latin.

————. *Institutes of the Christian Religion, 1536 Edition.* Revised edition. Translated by Ford Lewis Battles. Grand Rapids, Mich.: Wm. B. Eerdmans Publishing, 1986.

————. *The Mystery of Godliness and Other Selected Sermons.* Grand Rapids, Mich.: Wm. B. Eerdmans, 1950.

————. *Selected Works of John Calvin.* Edited by Jules Bonnet. Translated by David Constable. 7 vols. Grand Rapids, Mich.: Baker Book House, 1983.

————. *Selections From His Writings.* Edited with an Introduction by John Dillenberger. Missoula, Mont.: Scholars Press, 1975.

BOOKS AND ARTICLES ABOUT JOHN CALVIN

Bouwsma, William J. *John Calvin: A Sixteenth Century Portrait.* Oxford, England: Oxford University Press, 1988.

BIBLIOGRAPHY

Cooke, Charles L., M.D. "Calvin's Illnesses and Their Relation to Christian Vocation." In *Calvin Studies IV*. Edited by John Leith and W. Stacy Johnson. Davidson, N.C.: Davidson College, 1988, pp. 41–52.

Davis, Thomas J. *The Clearest Promises of God: The Development of Calvin's Eucharistic Teaching*. New York: AMS Press, 1995.

Ganoczy, Alexandre. *The Young Calvin*. Translated by David Foxgrover and Wade Provo. Philadelphia, Penn.: Westminster Press, 1987.

Gerrish, B.A. "John Calvin and the Reformed Doctrine of the Lord's Supper." In *McCormick Quarterly* 22 (1969): pp. 85–98.

Gerrish, Brian A. *Grace and Gratitude: The Eucharistic Theology of John Calvin*. Minneapolis, Minn.: Fortress Press, 1993.

Graham, W. Fred. *The Constructive Revolutionary: John Calvin and His Socio-Economic Impact*. Paperback edition. Atlanta, Ga.: John Knox Press, 1978.

McGrath, Alister E. *A Life of John Calvin: A Study in the Shaping of Western Culture*. Oxford, England: Basil Blackwell, 1990.

McNeill, John T. *The History and Character of Calvinism*. New York: Oxford University Press, 1954.

Naphy, William G. *Calvin and the Consolidation of the Genevan Reformation*. Louisville, Ky.: Westminster John Knox Press, 2003.

Parker, T.H.L. *John Calvin*. Paperback edition. Tring, England, and Batavia, Ill.: Lion Publishing, 1987.

van 't Spijker, Willem. "Calvin's Friendship with Martin Bucer." In *Calvin Studies Society Papers, 1995–1997: Calvin and Spirituality; Calvin and His Contemporaries*. Edited by David Foxgrover. Grand Rapids, Mich.: CSS, 1998, pp. 169–186.

BIBLIOGRAPHY

Wendel, François. *Calvin: The Origins and Development of His Religious Thought.* Translated by Philip Mairet. London: Wm. Collins Sons, 1963.

OTHER WORKS

The New Oxford Annotated Bible With the Apocrypha, Revised Standard Version. Edited by Herbert G. May and Bruce M. Metzger. New York: Oxford University Press, 1977.

Elwood, Christopher. *Calvin for Armchair Theologians*. Louisville, Ky.: Westminster John Knox Press, 2002.

McPherson, Joyce B. *The River of Grace: The Story of John Calvin*, 2nd ed. Lebanon, Tenn.: Greenleaf Press, 1998.

INDEX

accommodation, Calvin on, 29, 63, 64, 65, 66, 71, 76
Adam and Eve, Calvin on, 77
Agreement of Zurich, 49–50
Alberti, 19
Alciati, 22
anti-trinitarian, Servetus as, 58
anxiety, and sixteenth century, 5–7
Apostles' Creed, 28
Aquinas, St. Thomas, 81
Arianism, 35
Aristotle, Calvin studying, 18
Augustine, St., 81

baptism, 28, 29
    Calvin on, 44, 56, 69, 83
    Luther on, 16
Barth, Karl, 86
Basel, Switzerland
    Calvin returning to after Ferarra, 31
    Institutes of the Christian Religion completed in, 25–29
benefice
    Calvin obtaining, 12
    Calvin resigning, 24
Berthelier, Philibert, 54–56, 59
Beza, Theodore, 60
Bible
    authority of, 9, 44
    Calvin on, 65–67, 76, 78–79
    and humanism, 19
    and *Institutes of the Christian Religion*, 37
    and Protestantism, 14, 22, 23
    and University of Paris, 23.
    See also New Testament; Old Testament
blessed life, Calvin on, 76
Bolsec, Jerome, 53–54, 86
bubonic plague (black death), 9
Bucer, Martin, 49
Bullinger, Heinrich, 49, 50
Burckhardt, Jacob, 86

Calvin, Idelette de Bure (wife), 36, 51

Calvin, John
    and biblical commentaries, 37–38, 48, 64, 67, 70, 74, 94–95
    birth of, 12
    in Bourges, 22
    and Catholic Church, 12
    childhood of, 12–17
    children of, 51
    and choice for religious reform as Protestant, 3, 17, 22, 24–25
    as citizen of Geneva, 60
    and Cop's speech on reform, 23–24, 36
    death of, 4, 60–61
    and draft of ecclesiastical ordinances, 43, 44, 59
    education of, 12, 17–18, 20
    in exile from France, 14, 25, 31
    family of, 12, 18
    and financial concerns, 12, 22, 24
    and God's Word, 63–71
    and health problems, 50–51
    and humanism, 18–20, 22, 38
    as lawyer, 22
    legacy of, 4, 54, 73, 86–89
    and Luther, 87
    and marriage. *See* Calvin, Idelette de Bure
    and ministering to French refugees in Strasbourg, 36–39, 42–43, 49
    in Noyon, 12, 22–23, 24
    and obtaining benefice, 12
    in Orléans, 18, 22
    in Paris, 17–18, 22, 23
    and personality, 31
    and private studies, 3, 4
    and resigning benefice, 24
    in Switzerland. *See* Basel, Switzerland; Geneva, Switzerland
    as theocrat, 55–56
    theology of, 26–28, 36–39, 43–48, 53–54. *See also Institutes of the Christian Religion*
    as villain, 54, 56–59, 87

INDEX

and *Institutes of the Christian Religion,* 73
Luther on, 15–16
and Paul, 37–38
Savoyard rule, and Geneva, Switzerland, 32
Saxony, and Luther, 31–32
Scandinavian countries, Lutheranism in, 87
Scotland, Calvinism in, 88
"Scripture Alone!", 67
Scripture readings, Calvin on in Geneva, 44
second-generation reformer, Calvin as, 17
Seneca, 5
and Calvin's commentary on *On Clemency* of, 4, 22
sermons, Calvin on in Geneva, 44
"Sermons on the Saving Work of Christ," 98–101
Servetus, Michael, 56–59
Short Treatise on the Holy Supper of Our Lord Jesus Christ, A, 39, 49–50, 96–97
"siege" mentality, in sixteenth century, 7
sin. *See* original sin
sixteenth century
and anxiety, 5–7
and religious upheaval and uncertainty, 7–10
social services, in Geneva, 47–48
soul, Calvin on, 76–77
South Africa, Calvinism in, 88
South Korea, Calvinism in, 88
Spain
and heretics, 57
and Inquisition, 57
Süleyman the Magnificent, 7
Switzerland
and Berne, 32, 35
Calvinism in, 88

and Zurich, 35, 49–50.
See also Basel, Switzerland; Geneva, Switzerland

teachers, Calvin on in Geneva, 44
Ten Commandments
Calvin on, 66, 78
in *Institutes of the Christian Religion,* 26–28
theologian, 73
Calvin as, 26–28, 36–39, 43–48, 53–54. *See also Institutes of the Christian Religion*
Trinity, Calvin on, 76

understanding (intellect), Calvin on, 77–78
United States, and Calvinism, 86, 88, 88–89
United States Constitution, and Calvin, 88
University of Geneva, 48, 60
University of Paris
and Calvin at Collège de Montaigu, 18
and Cop's inaugural speech on reform, 23–24, 36
and humanism, 23
and Luther, 23

Vienna, and Servetus, 58

will, Calvin on, 77–78
Winthrop, John, 89
Wittenberg, Saxony, and Ninety-Five Theses, 15
worship service, Calvin on in Geneva, 43–44

Zwingli, Ulrich, 49
Zwinglians, and communion, 70

ABOUT THE CONTRIBUTORS

THOMAS J. DAVIS received his Ph.D. from the University of Chicago in 1992. He currently serves as Chairperson of the Department of Religious Studies at Indiana University-Purdue University, Indianapolis. He is a Fellow of the International Congress for Calvin Research, and he has written extensively on John Calvin. He has served as Managing Editor of *Religion and American Culture: A Journal of Interpretation* since 1989. He also writes novels.

Davis dedicates this book to his friend, colleague, and mentor, Rowland A. "Tony" Sherrill (1944–2003), who was also a one-time Chelsea House author.

MARTIN E. MARTY is an ordained minister in the Evangelical Lutheran Church and the Fairfax M. Cone Distinguished Service Professor Emeritus at the University of Chicago Divinity School, where he taught for thirty-five years. Marty has served as president of the American Academy of Religion, the American Society of Church History, and the American Catholic Historical Association, and was also a member of two U.S. presidential commissions. He is currently Senior Regent at St. Olaf College in Northfield, Minnesota. Marty has written more than fifty books, including the three-volume *Modern American Religion* (University of Chicago Press). His book *Righteous Empire* was a recipient of the National Book Award.